# TRUE HARVEST

# TRUE HARVEST

*Readings from Henry David Thoreau for Every Day of the Year*

COLLECTED BY
**BARRY ANDREWS**

SKINNER HOUSE BOOKS
BOSTON

Cover art by Irma Cerese, *World's End #4*, acrylic on canvas, 16 x 16", www.ceresearts.com
Cover design by Gopa & Ted2, Inc.
Text design by Suzanne Morgan.

Printed in the United States.

ISBN 1-55896-490-8
978-1-55896-490-7

10 9 8 7 6 5 4 3 2 1
07 06 05

Library of Congress Cataloging-in-Publication Data

Thoreau, Henry David, 1817-1862.
    True harvest : readings from Henry David Thoreau for every day of the year / collected by Barry M. Andrews.
        p. cm.
    ISBN 1-55896-490-8 (alk. paper)
    1. Meditations. 2. Spiritual life. 3. Conduct of life. I. Andrews, Barry Maxwell. II. Title.

BL624.2.T48 2005
818'.309--dc22                                        2005021985

The true harvest of my daily life is somewhat as intangible and indescribable as the tints of morning or evening. It is a little star-dust caught, a segment of the rainbow which I have clutched.

Henry David Thoreau

# INTRODUCTION

The year 2004 marked the 150th anniversary of Henry David Thoreau's *Walden*, first published in August 1854. The milestone was greeted with articles in local newspapers and national magazines and the publication of several new editions of the classic, adding to the hundreds of others published in the years since the author's death.

The attention given to the event indicates the high esteem in which American culture holds Thoreau, primarily as a social critic and champion of the environment. Thousands of people from all over the world make annual pilgrimages to Walden Pond, famous for the two years Thoreau lived in a small cabin on its shores.

Thoreau was a person of many interests, none greater than reading, writing, and sauntering in the woods and fields surrounding his native Concord. He was a keen observer not only of the natural world but of politics and social life as well. His observations on nature and society enter into all of his writings, filtered through the lens of his uniquely religious and philosophical point of view.

In many ways it is easier to appreciate Thoreau in our day than it was in his own. To a large degree the world has come around to his point of view on many issues, including civil disobedience, simple living, and stewardship of the environment. Although his religious views are still unconventional by today's standards, they nevertheless have wide appeal too. Thoreau's interest in Asian religions is shared by many people today and his emphasis on nature and everyday spirituality is in keeping with a growing trend in American religious life.

Thoreau is among the most quoted of American writers. *Walden* alone contains dozens of well-known sayings, including such memorable quotations as "beware of enterprises that require new clothes," "the mass of men live lives of quiet desperation," and perhaps most familiar of all: "If a man does not keep pace with his companions, perhaps it is because he hears a different drummer."

The selections chosen for this collection reflect the broad range of Thoreau's interests, and they are taken from the whole of his writings—his letters and journals as well as his lectures, essays, and books. Preference has been given here to longer passages in which he develops a thought and sees it through to its conclusion. Sublime and volatile truths, these passages are intended to be read and reflected upon as meditations for each day of the year.

Thoreau is sometimes criticized as a solitary mystic who preferred a life in the woods to active engagement with the world of his time. Nothing could be further from the truth, as many of these words will reveal. Thoreau realized that spiritual growth does not take place in total isolation and that social, economic, and political conditions affect us all.

In *Walden* Thoreau tells us that he desires to wake up his neighbors. It is not his intention that people should adopt his mode of living, he writes. They should find and pursue their own way, not their father's or their mother's or someone else's. He means to be provocative, to be "*extra*-vagant," to wander out of bounds, as it were. Thoreau summons us to the spiritual life. He is a wake-up call to greater awareness.

JANUARY

## JANUARY 1

Men nowhere, east or west, live yet a *natural* life, round which the vine clings, and which the elm willingly shadows. Man would desecrate it by his touch, and so the beauty of the world remains veiled to him. He needs not only to be spiritualized, but *naturalized*, on the soil of earth. Who shall conceive what kind of roof the heavens might extend over him, what seasons minister to him, and what employment dignify his life! Only the convalescent raises the veil of nature. An immortality in his life would confer immortality on his abode. The winds should be his breath, the seasons his moods, and he should impart of his serenity to Nature herself. But such as we know him he is ephemeral like the scenery which surrounds him, and does not aspire to an enduring existence. When we come down into the distant village, visible from the mountain-top, the nobler inhabitants with whom we peopled it have departed, and left only vermin in its desolate streets. . . . Here or nowhere is our heaven.

A WEEK ON THE CONCORD & MERRIMACK RIVERS

## JANUARY 2

Here is this vast, savage, howling Mother of ours, Nature, lying all around, with such beauty, and such affection for her children, as the leopard; and yet we are so early weaned from her breast to society, to that culture which is exclusively an interaction of man on man,—a sort of breeding in and in, which produces at most a merely

English nobility, a civilization destined to have a speedy limit. In society, in the best institutions of men it is easy to detect a certain precocity. When we should still be growing children, we are already little men. Give me a culture which imports much muck from the meadows, and deepens the soil, not that which trusts to heating manures, and improved implements and modes of culture only. . . . I would not have every man nor every part of a man cultivated, any more than I would have every acre of earth cultivated; part will be tillage, but the greater part will be meadow and forest, not only serving an immediate use, but preparing a mould against a distant future, by the annual decay of the vegetation which it supports.

WALKING

## JANUARY 3

I love Nature partly *because* she is not man, but a retreat from him. None of his institutions control or pervade her. There a different kind of right prevails. In her midst I can be glad with an entire gladness. If this world were all man, I could not stretch myself, I should lose all hope. He is constraint, she is freedom to me. He makes me wish for another world. She makes me content with this. None of the joys she supplies is subject to his rules and definitions. What he touches he taints. In thought he moralizes. One would think that no free, joyful labor was possible to him. How infinite and pure the least pleasure of which Nature is basis, compared with the

congratulation of mankind! The joy which Nature yields
is like [that] afforded by the frank words of one we love.

## JANUARY 4

A man receives only what he is ready to receive, whether
physically or intellectually or morally, as animals conceive at certain seasons their kind only. We hear and
apprehend only what we already half know. If there is
something which does not concern me, which is out of
my line, which by experience or by genius my attention
is not drawn to, however novel and remarkable it may
be, if it is spoken we hear it not, if it is written, we read
it not, or if we read it, it does not detain us. Every man
thus *tracks himself* through life, in all his hearing and
reading and observation and travelling. His observations
make a chain. The phenomenon or fact that cannot in
any wise be linked with the rest which he has observed,
he does not observe. By and by we may be ready to
receive what we cannot receive now.

## JANUARY 5

Is it the source of the Nile, or the Niger, or the Mississippi, or a Northwest Passage around this continent,
that we would find? Are these the problems which most
concern mankind? Is Franklin the only man who is lost,
that his wife should be so earnest to find him? Does

Mr. Grinnell know where he himself is? Be rather the Mungo Park, the Lewis and Clarke and Frobisher, of your own streams and oceans; explore your own higher latitudes. . . . Nay, be a Columbus to whole new continents and worlds within you, opening new channels, not of trade, but of thought. Every man is the lord of a realm beside which the earthly empire of the Czar is but a petty state, a hummock left by the ice. Yet some can be patriotic who have no *self-respect*, and sacrifice the greater to the less. They love the soil which makes their graves, but have no sympathy with the spirit which may still animate their clay. . . . What was the meaning of that South-Sea Exploring Expedition, with all its parade and expense, but an indirect recognition of the fact that there are continents and seas in the moral world to which every man is an isthmus or an inlet, yet unexplored by him, but that it is easier to sail many thousand miles through cold and storm and cannibals, in a government ship, with five hundred men and boys to assist one, than it is to explore the private sea, the Atlantic and Pacific Ocean of one's being alone.

WALDEN

## JANUARY 6

I was feeling very cheap, nevertheless, reduced to make the most of dry dogwood berries. Very little evidence of God or man did I see just then, and life not as rich and inviting an enterprise as it should be, when my attention was caught by a snowflake on my coat-sleeve. It was one of those perfect, crystalline, star-shaped ones, six-rayed, like a flat wheel with six spokes, only the spokes were perfect little pine trees in shape, arranged around a central spangle. This little object, which, with many of its fellows, rested unmelting on my coat, so perfect and beautiful, reminded me that Nature had not lost her pristine vigor yet, and why should man lose heart? . . . These little wheels came down like the wrecks of chariots from a battle waged in the sky. There were mingled with these starry flakes small downy pellets also. . . . We are rained and snowed on with gems. I confess that I was a little encouraged, for I was beginning to believe that Nature was poor and mean, and I was now convinced that she turned off as good work as ever. What a world we live in! Where are the jewellers' shops? There is nothing handsomer than a snowflake and a dewdrop. I may say that the maker of the world exhausts his skill with each snowflake and dewdrop that he sends down. We think that the one mechanically coheres and that the other simply flows together and falls, but in truth they are the product of *enthusiasm*, the children of an ecstasy, finished with the artist's utmost skill.

JOURNAL 1858

## JANUARY 7

There is nothing so sanative, so poetic, as a walk in the woods and fields even now, when I meet none abroad for pleasure. Nothing so inspires me and excites such serene and profitable thought. The objects are elevating. In the street and in society I am almost invariably cheap and dissipated, my life is unspeakably mean. No amount of gold or respectability would in the least redeem it,— dining with the Governor or a member of Congress!! But alone in distant woods or fields, in unpretending sprout-lands or pastures tracked by rabbits, even in a bleak and, to most, cheerless day, like this, when a villager would be thinking of his inn, I come to myself. I once more feel myself grandly related, and that cold and solitude are friends of mine. I suppose that this value, in my case, is equivalent to what others get by churchgoing and prayer. I come to my solitary woodland walk as the homesick go home. I thus dispose of the superfluous and see things as they are, grand and beautiful. I have told many that I walk every day about half the daylight, but I think they do not believe it. I wish to get the Concord, the Massachusetts, the America, out of my head and be sane a part of every day. If there are missionaries for the heathen, why not send them to me? I wish to know something; I wish to be made better. I wish to forget, a considerable part of every day, all mean, narrow, trivial men . . . and therefore I come out to these solitudes, where the problem of existence is simplified. I get away a mile or two from the town into the stillness and solitude of nature, with rocks, trees, weeds, snow about me. I enter some glade in the woods, perchance, where a few weeds and dry leaves alone lift themselves above the surface of the snow, and it is as if I had come to an open window. I see out and around myself. Our *skylights* are thus far away from the ordinary resorts of men. I am not satisfied with ordinary windows. I must have a true *skylight*. My true skylight is on the outside of the village.

## JANUARY 8

It would be worth the while to select our reading, for books are the society we keep; to read only the serenely true; never statistics, nor fiction, nor news, nor reports, nor periodicals, but only great poems, and when they failed, read them again, or perchance write more. Instead of other sacrifice, we might offer up our perfect . . . thoughts to the gods daily, in hymns or psalms. For we should be at the helm at least once a day. The whole of the day should not be daytime; there should be one hour, if no more, which the day did not bring forth. Scholars are wont to sell their birthright for a mess of learning. . . . Read the best books first, or you may not have a chance to read them at all. . . . Books, not which afford us a cowering enjoyment, but in which each thought is of unusual daring; such as an idle man cannot read, and a timid one would not be entertained by, which even make us dangerous to existing institutions,—such call I good books.

A WEEK ON THE CONCORD & MERRIMACK RIVERS

## JANUARY 9

There are from time to time mornings, both in summer and winter, when especially the world seems to begin anew, beyond which memory need not go, for not behind them is yesterday and our past life; when, as in the morning of a hoar frost, there are visible the effects of a certain creative energy, the world has visibly been recreated in the night. Mornings of creation, I call them. In the midst of these marks of a creative energy recently active, while the sun is rising with more than usual splendor, I look back,—I look back for the era of this creation, not into the night, but to a dawn for which no man ever rose early enough. A morning which carries us back beyond the Mosaic creation, where crystallizations are fresh and unmelted. It is the poet's hour. Mornings when men are new-born, men who have the seeds of life in them. It should be a part of my religion to be abroad then.

## JANUARY 10

What are the natural features which make a township handsome? A river, with its waterfalls and meadows, a lake, a hill, a cliff or individual rocks, a forest, and ancient trees standing singly. Such things are beautiful; they have a high use which dollars and cents never represent. If the inhabitants of a town were wise, they would seek to preserve these things, though at a considerable expense; for such things educate far more than any hired teachers or preachers, or any at present recognized system of school education. I do not think him fit to be the founder of a state or even of a town who does not foresee the use of these things, but legislates chiefly for oxen, as it were. . . . But most men, it seems to me, do not care for Nature and would sell their share in all her beauty, as long as they may live, for a stated sum—many for a glass of rum. Thank God, men cannot as yet fly, and lay waste to the sky as well as the earth! We are safe on that side for the present. It is for the very reason that some do not care for those things that we need to continue to protect all from the vandalism of the few.

JOURNAL 1861

## JANUARY 11

With thinking we may be beside ourselves in a sane sense. By a conscious effort of the mind we can stand aloof from actions and their consequences; and all things, good and bad, go by us like a torrent. We are not wholly involved in Nature. I may be either the driftwood in the stream, or Indra in the sky looking down on it. I *may* be affected by a theatrical exhibition; on the other hand, I *may not* be affected by an actual event which appears to concern me much more. I only know myself as a human entity; the scene, so to speak, of thoughts and affections; and am sensible of a certain doubleness by which I can stand as remote from myself as from another. However intense my experience, I am conscious of the presence and criticism of a part of me, which, as it were, is not a part of me, but spectator, sharing no experience, but taking note of it; and that is no more I than it is you. When the play, it may be the tragedy, of life is over, the spectator goes his way. It was a kind of fiction, a work of the imagination only, so far as he was concerned. This doubleness may easily make us poor neighbors and friends sometimes.

## JANUARY 12

I sometimes think that I may go forth and walk hard and earnestly, and live a more substantial life and get a glorious experience; be much abroad in heat and cold, day and night; live more, expend more atmospheres, be weary often, etc., etc. But then swiftly the thought comes to me, Go not so far out of your way for a truer life; keep strictly onward in that path alone which your genius points out. Do the things which lie nearest to you, but which are difficult to do. Live a purer, a more thoughtful and laborious life, more true to your friends and neighbors, more noble and magnanimous, and that will be better than a wild walk.

## JANUARY 13

I hear one thrumming a guitar below stairs. It reminds me of moments that I have lived. What a comment on our life is the least strain of music! It lifts me above all the dust and mire of the universe. I soar and hover with clean skirts over the field of my life. It is ever life within life, in concentric spheres. . . . The identical field where I am leading my humdrum life, let but a strain of music be heard there, is seen to be the field of some unrecorded crusade or tournament the thought of which excites in us an ecstasy of joy. The way in which I am affected by this faint thrumming advertises me that there is still some health and immortality in the springs of me. . . . I am, of course, hopelessly ignorant and unbelieving until some divinity stirs within me. Ninety-nine one-hundredths of our lives we are mere hedgers and ditchers, but from time to time we meet with reminders of our destiny. We hear the kindred vibrations, music! and we put out our dormant feelers unto the limits of the universe. We attain to a wisdom that passeth understanding. The stable continents undulate. The hard and fixed becomes fluid. . . . When I *hear* music I fear no danger, I am invulnerable, I see no foe. I am related to the earliest times and to the latest. There are infinite degrees of life, from that which is next to sleep and death, to that which is forever awake and immortal. . . . I am constrained to believe that the mass of men are never so lifted above themselves that their destiny is seen to be transcendentally beautiful and grand.

JOURNAL 1857

## JANUARY 14

The chief want, in every State that I have been into, was a high and earnest purpose in its inhabitants. This alone draws out "the great resources" of Nature, and at last taxes her beyond her resources; for man naturally dies out of her. When we want culture more than potatoes, and illumination more than sugar-plums, then the great resources of a world are taxed and drawn out, and the result, or staple production, is, not slaves, nor operatives, but men,—those rare fruits called heroes, saints, poets, philosophers, and redeemers.

LIFE WITHOUT PRINCIPLE

## JANUARY 15

What is there in music that it should so stir our deeps? We are all ordinarily in a state of desperation; such is our life; ofttimes it drives us to suicide. . . . But let us hear a strain of music, we are at once advertised of a life which no man had told us of, which no preacher preaches. Suppose I try to describe faithfully the prospect which a strain of music exhibits to me. The field of my life becomes a boundless plain, glorious to tread, with no death nor disappointment at the end of it. All meanness and trivialness disappear. I become adequate to any deed. No particulars survive this expansion; persons do not survive it. In the light of this strain there is no thou nor I. We are actually above ourselves.

JOURNAL 1857

 ## JANUARY 16

Why should we live with such hurry and waste of life? We are determined to be starved before we are hungry. Men say that a stitch in time saves nine, and so they take a thousand stitches to-day to save nine to-morrow. As for *work*, we haven't any of any consequence. We have the Saint Vitus' dance, and cannot possibly keep our heads still. . . . Hardly a man takes a half hour's nap after dinner, but when he wakes he holds up his head and asks, "What's the news?" as if the rest of mankind had stood his sentinels. Some give directions to be waked every half hour, doubtless for no other purpose; and then, to pay for it, they tell what they have dreamed. After a night's sleep the news is as indispensable as the breakfast. "Pray tell me any thing new that has happened to a man any where on this globe"—and he reads it over his coffee and rolls, that a man has had his eyes gouged out this morning on the Wachito River; never dreaming the while that he lives in the dark unfathomed mammoth cave of this world, and has but the rudiment of an eye himself.

WALDEN


## JANUARY 17

In proportion as I have celestial thoughts, is the necessity for me to be out and behold the western sky before sunset these winter days. That is the symbol of the unclouded mind that knows neither winter nor summer. What is your thought like? That is the hue, that the purity, and transparency, and distance from earthly taint of my inmost mind, for whatever we see without is a symbol of something within, and that which is farthest off is the symbol of what is deepest within. The lover of contemplation, accordingly, will gaze much into the sky. Fair thoughts and a serene mind will make fair days. The rainbow is the symbol of the triumph which succeeds to a grief that has tried us to our advantage, so that at last we can smile through our tears. It is the aspect with which we come out of the house of mourning. We have found our relief in tears. As the skies appear to a man, so is his mind. Some see only clouds there; some, prodigies and portents; some rarely look up at all; their heads, like the brutes', are directed toward earth. Some behold there serenity, purity, beauty ineffable. The world run to see the panorama, when there is a panorama in the sky which few go out to see.

JOURNAL 1852

## JANUARY 18

We are accustomed to say, that the mass of men are unprepared; but improvement is slow, because the few are not materially wiser or better than the many. It is not so important that many should be as good as you, as that there be some absolute goodness somewhere; for that will leaven the whole lump. There are thousands who are *in opinion* opposed to slavery and to the war, who yet in effect do nothing to put an end to them; who, esteeming themselves children of Washington and Franklin, sit down with their hands in their pockets, and say that they not know what to do, and do nothing; who even postpone the question of freedom to the question of free-trade, and quietly read the prices—current along with the latest advices from Mexico, after dinner, and, it may be, fall asleep over them both. What is the price-current of an honest man and patriot to-day?

RESISTANCE TO CIVIL GOVERNMENT

## JANUARY 19

As I walk the railroad causeway I am, as the last two months, disturbed by the sound of my steps on the frozen ground. I wish to hear the silence of the night, for the silence is something positive and to be heard. I cannot walk with my ears covered. I must stand still and listen with open ears, far from the noises of the village, that the night may make its impression on me. A fertile and eloquent silence. Sometimes the silence is merely negative, and arid and barren waste in which I shudder, where no ambrosia grows. I must hear the whispering of a myriad voices. Silence alone is worthy to be heard. Silence is of various depth and fertility, like soil. Now it is a mere Sahara, where men perish of hunger and thirst, now a fertile bottom, or prairie, of the West. As I leave the village, drawing nearer to the woods, I listen from time to time to hear the sounds of Silence baying the moon,—to know if they are on the track of any game. If there's no Diana in the night, what is it worth? I hark the goddess Diana. The silence rings; it is musical and thrills me. A night in which the silence was audible. I hear the unspeakable.

## JANUARY 20

It may be guessed that I reduce almost the whole advantage of holding this superfluous property as a fund in store against the future, so far as the individual is concerned, mainly to the defraying of funeral expenses. But perhaps a man is not required to bury himself. Nevertheless this points to an important distinction between the civilized man and the savage; and, no doubt, they have designs on us for our benefit, in making the life of a civilized people an *institution*, in which the life of the individual is to a great extent absorbed, in order to preserve and perfect that of the race. But I wish to show at what a sacrifice this advantage is at present obtained, and to suggest that we may possibly so live as to secure all the advantage without suffering any of the disadvantage. What mean ye by saying that the poor ye have always with you, or that the fathers have eaten sour grapes, and the children's teeth are set on edge?

WALDEN

## JANUARY 21

Every leaf and twig was this morning covered with a sparkling ice armor; even the grasses in exposed fields were hung with innumerable diamond pendants, which jingled merrily when brushed by the foot of the traveller. It was literally the wreck of jewels and the crash of gems. It was as though some superincumbent stratum of the earth had been removed in the night, exposing to light a bed of untarnished crystals. The scene changed at every step, or as the head was inclined to the right or left. There were the opal and sapphire and emerald and jasper and beryl and topaz and ruby. Such is beauty ever,—neither here nor there, now nor then,—neither in Rome nor Athens, but wherever there is a soul to admire. If I seek her elsewhere because I do not find her at home, my search will prove a fruitless one.

JOURNAL 1838

## JANUARY 22

To set down such choice experiences that my own writings may inspire me and at last I may make wholes of parts. Certainly it is a distinct profession to rescue from oblivion and to fix the sentiments and thoughts which visit all more or less generally, that the contemplation of the unfinished picture may suggest its harmonious completion. Associate reverently and as much as you can with your loftiest thoughts. Each thought that is welcomed and recorded is a nest egg, by the side of which more will be laid. Thoughts accidentally thrown together become a frame in which more may be developed and exhibited. Perhaps this is the main value of a habit of writing, of keeping a journal,—that so we remember our best hours and stimulate ourselves. My thoughts are my company. They have a certain individuality and separate existence, aye, personality. Having by chance recorded a few disconnected thoughts and then brought them into juxtaposition, they suggest a whole new field in which it

was possible to labor and to think. Thought begat
thought.

## JANUARY 23

When we walk, we naturally go to the fields and woods;
what would become of us if we walked only in a garden or
a mall? . . . Of course, it is of no use to direct our steps to
the woods, if they do not carry us thither. I am alarmed
when it happens that I have walked a mile into the woods
bodily, without getting there in spirit. In my afternoon
walk I would fain forget all my morning occupations, and
my obligations to society. But it sometimes happens that
I cannot easily shake off the village. The thought of some
work will run in my head, and I am not where my body is;
I am out of my senses. In my walks I would fain return to
my senses. What business have I in the woods, if I am
thinking of something out of the woods?

WALKING

## JANUARY 24

Improve each occasion when thy soul is reached. Drain
the cup of inspiration to its last dregs. Fear no intemperance in that, for the years will come when otherwise
thou wilt regret opportunities unimproved. The spring
will not last forever. These fertile and expanding seasons
of thy life, when the rain reaches thy root, when thy vigor
shoots, when thy flower is budding, shall be fewer and

farther between. Again I say, Remember thy Creator in the days of thy youth. Use and commit to life what you cannot commit to memory. I hear the tones of my sister's piano below. It reminds me of strains which I once heard more frequently, when, possessed with the inaudible rhythm, I sought my chamber in the cold and communed with my own thoughts. I feel as if I then received the gifts of the gods with too much indifference. Why did I not cultivate those fields they introduced me to? Does nothing withstand the inevitable march of time? Why did I not use my eyes when I stood on Pisgah? Now I hear those strains but seldom. My rhythmical mood does not endure. I cannot draw from it and return to it in my thought as to a well all the evening or the morning. I cannot dip my pen in it. I cannot work the vein, it is so fine and volatile. Ah, sweet, ineffable reminiscences!

JOURNAL 1852

## JANUARY 25

Merely to come into the world the heir of a fortune is not to be born, but to be still-born, rather. To be supported by the charity of friends, or a government pension,—provided you continue to breathe,—by whatever fine synonyms you describe these relations, is to go into the almshouse. On Sundays the poor debtor goes to church to take an account of stock, and finds, of course, that his outgoes have been greater than his income. In the Catholic Church, especially, they go into chancery, make a clean confession, give up all, and think to start again. Thus men will lie on their backs, talking about the fall of man, and never make an effort to get up.

LIFE WITHOUT PRINCIPLE

## JANUARY 26

Obey the spur of the moment. These accumulated it is that make the impulse and the impetus of the life of genius. These are the spongioles or rootlets by which its trunk is fed. If you neglect the moments, if you cut off your fibrous roots, what but a languishing life is to be expected? Let the spurs of countless moments goad us incessantly into life. I feel the spur of the moment thrust deep into my side. The present is an inexorable rider. The moment always spurs either with a sharp or a blunt spur. Are my sides calloused? Let us trust the rider, that he knows the way, that he knows when speed and effort are required. What other impulse do we wait for? Let us preserve religiously, secure, protect the coincidence of our life with the life of nature. Else what are heat and cold, day and night, sun, moon, and stars to us? Was it not from sympathy with the present life of nature that we were born at this epoch rather than at another?

JOURNAL 1852

## JANUARY 27

I have some good friends from whom I am wont to part with disappointment, for they neither care what I think nor mind what I say. The greatest compliment that was ever paid me was when one asked me what I *thought*, and attended to my answer. We begin to die, not in our senses or extremities, but in our divine faculties. Our members may be sound, our sight and hearing perfect, but our genius and imagination betray signs of decay. You tell me that you are growing old and are troubled to see without glasses, but this is unimportant if the divine faculty of the seer shows no signs of decay.

## JANUARY 28

Our life should be so active and progressive as to be a journey. Our meals should all be of journey-cake and hasty pudding. We should be more alert, see the sun rise, not keep fashionable hours, enter a house, our own house, as a khan, a caravansary. At noon I did not dine; I ate my journey-cake. I quenched my thirst at a spring or a brook. As I sat at the table, the hospitality was so perfect and the repast so sumptuous that I seemed to be breaking my fast upon a bank in the midst of an arduous journey, that the water seemed to be a living spring, the napkins grass, the conversation free as the winds; and the servants that waited on us were our simple desires.

## JANUARY 29

Of all the strange and unaccountable things this journalizing is the strangest. It will allow nothing to be predicted of it; its good is not good, nor its bad bad. If I make a huge effort to expose my innermost and richest wares to light, my counter seems cluttered with the meanest homemade stuffs; but after months or years I may discover the wealth of India, and whatever rarity is brought overland from Cathay, in that confused heap, and what perhaps seemed a festoon of dried apple or pumpkin will prove a string of Brazilian diamonds, or pearls from Coromandel.

## JANUARY 30

I tread in the tracks of the fox which has gone before me by some hours, or which perhaps I have started, with such a tiptoe of expectation as if I were on the trail of the Spirit itself which resides in these woods, and expected soon to catch it in its lair. The snow falls on no two trees alike, but the forms it assumes are as various as those of the twigs and leaves which receive it. They are, as it were, predetermined by the genius of the tree. So one divine spirit descends alike on all, but bears a particular fruit in each. The divinity subsides on all men, as the snowflakes settle on the fields and ledges and takes the form of the various clefts and surfaces in which it lodges.

The winter, cold and bound out as it is, is thrown to us like a bone to a famishing dog, and we are expected to get the marrow out of it. . . . Some desert the field and go into winter quarters in the city. They attend the oratorios, while the only music that we countrymen hear is the squeaking of the snow under our boots. But the winter was not given to us for no purpose. We must thaw its cold with our genialness. We are tasked to find out and appropriate all the nutriment it yields. If it is a cold and hard season, its fruit, no doubt, is the more concentrated and nutty. It took the cold and bleakness of November to ripen the walnut, but the human brain is the kernel which the winter itself matures. Not till then does its shell come off. The seasons were not made in vain. Because the fruits of the earth are already ripe, we are not to suppose that there is no fruit left for winter to ripen. It is for man the seasons and all their fruits exist. The winter was made to concentrate and harden and mature the kernel of his brain, to give tone and firmness and consistency to his thought. Then is the great harvest of the year, the harvest of thought. All previous harvests are stubble to this, mere fodder and green crop.

JOURNAL 1854

FEBRUARY

## FEBRUARY 1

After a still winter night I awoke with the impression that some question had been put to me, which I had been endeavoring in vain to answer in my sleep, as what—how—when—where? But there was dawning Nature, in whom all creatures live, looking in at my broad windows with serene and satisfied face, and no question on *her* lips. I awoke to an unanswered question, to Nature and daylight. The snow lying deep on the earth dotted with young pines, and the very slope of the hill on which my house is placed, seemed to say, Forward! Nature puts no question and answers none which we mortals ask. She has long ago taken her resolution. "O Prince, our eyes contemplate with admiration and transmit to the soul the wonderful and varied spectacle of this universe. The night veils without doubt a part of this glorious creation; but day comes to reveal to us this great work, which extends from earth even into the plains of the ether."

WALDEN

## FEBRUARY 2

Men rush to California and Australia as if the true gold were to be found in that direction; but that is to go to the very opposite extreme to where it lies. They go prospecting farther and farther away from the true lead, and are most unfortunate when they think themselves most successful. Is not our *native* soil auriferous? Does not a stream from the golden mountains flow through our native valley? and has not this for more than geologic ages been bringing down the shining particles and forming the nuggets for us? Yet, strange to tell, if a digger steal away, prospecting for this true gold, into the unexplored solitudes around us, there is no danger that any will dog his steps, and endeavor to supplant him. He may claim and undermine the whole valley even, both the cultivated and the uncultivated portions, his whole life long in peace, for no one will ever dispute his claim.

LIFE WITHOUT PRINCIPLE

## FEBRUARY 3

It is the spirit of humanity, that which animates both so-called savages and civilized nations, working through a man, and not the man expressing himself, that interests us most. The thought of a so-called savage tribe is generally far more just than that of a single civilized man. I perceive that we partially die ourselves through sympathy at the death of each of our friends or near relatives. Each such experience is an assault on our vital force. It becomes a source of wonder that they who have lost many friends still live. After long watching around the sick-bed of a friend, we, too, partially give up the ghost with him, and are the less to be identified with this state of things.

JOURNAL 1859

## FEBRUARY 4

I sometimes hear a prominent but dull-witted worthy man say . . . that if it were not for his firm belief in "an overruling power," or a "perfect Being," etc., etc. But such poverty-stricken expressions only convince me of his habitual doubt and that he is surprised into a transient belief. Such a man's expression of faith, moving solemnly in the traditional furrow, and casting out all free-thinking and living souls with the rusty mould-board of his compassion or contempt, thinking that he has Moses and all the prophets in his wake, discourages and saddens me as an expression of his narrow and barren want of faith. I see that the infidels and skeptics have formed themselves into churches and weekly gather together at the ringing of a bell . . . So, when I have been resting and quenching my thirst on the eternal plains of truth, where rests the base of those beautiful columns that sustain the heavens, I have been amused to see a traveller who had long confined himself to the quaking shore, which was all covered with the traces of the deluge, come timidly tiptoeing toward me, trembling in every limb.

JOURNAL 1857

## FEBRUARY 5

I desire to speak somewhere *without* bounds; like a man in a waking moment, to men in their waking moments; for I am convinced that I cannot exaggerate enough even to lay the foundation of a true expression. Who that has heard a strain of music feared then lest he should speak extravagantly any more forever? In view of the future or possible, we should live quite laxly and undefined in front, our outlines dim and misty on that side; as our shadows reveal an insensible perspiration toward the sun. The volatile truth of our words should continually betray the inadequacy of the residual statement. Their truth is instantly *translated*; its literal monument alone remains. The words which express our faith and piety are not definite; yet they are significant and fragrant like frankincense to superior natures.

WALDEN

## FEBRUARY 6

Under a government which imprisons any unjustly, the true place for a just man is also a prison. The proper place to-day, the only place which Massachusetts has provided for her freer and less desponding spirits, is in her prisons, to be put out and locked out of the State by her own act, as they have already put themselves out by their principles. It is there that the fugitive slave, and the Mexican prisoner on parole, and the Indian come to plead the wrongs of his race, should find them; on that separate but more free and honorable ground, where the State places those who are not *with* her, but *against* her,—the only house in a slave State in which a free man can abide with honor. If any think that their influence would be lost there, and their voices no longer afflict the ear of the State, that they would not be as an enemy within its walls, they do not know by how much truth is stronger than error, nor how much more eloquently and effectively he can combat injustice who has experienced a little in his own person.

RESISTANCE TO CIVIL GOVERNMENT

## FEBRUARY 7

If I could, I would worship the parings of my nails. If he who makes two blades of grass grow where one grew before is a benefactor, he who discovers two gods where there was only known the one (and such a one!) before is a still greater benefactor. I would fain improve every opportunity to wonder and worship, as a sunflower welcomes the light. The more thrilling, wonderful, divine objects I behold in a day, the more expanded and immortal I become. If a stone appeals to me and elevates me, tells me how many miles I have come, how many remain to travel—and the more, the better—reveals the future to me in some measure, it is a matter of private rejoicing.

JOURNAL 1856

## FEBRUARY 8

My Journal is that of me which would else spill over and run to waste, gleanings from the field which in action I reap. I must not live for it, but in it for the gods. They are my correspondent, to whom daily I send off this sheet postpaid. I am clerk in their counting-room, and at evening transfer the account from day-book to ledger. It is as a leaf that hangs over my head in the path. I bend the twig and write my prayers on it; then letting it go, the bough springs up and shows the scrawl to heaven. As if it were not kept shut in my desk, but were as public a leaf as any in nature. It is papyrus by the riverside; it is vellum in the pastures; it is parchment on the hills. I find it everywhere as free as the leaves which troop along the lanes in autumn. The crow, the goose, the eagle carry my quill, and the wind blows the leaves as far as I go. Or, if my imagination does not soar, but gropes in slime and mud, then I write with a reed.

JOURNAL 1841

## FEBRUARY 9

The mass of men lead lives of quiet desperation. What is called resignation is confirmed desperation. From the desperate city you go into the desperate country, and have to console yourself with the bravery of minks and muskrats. A stereotyped but unconscious despair is concealed even under what are called the games and amusements of mankind. There is no play in them, for this comes after work. But it is a characteristic of wisdom not to do desperate things. . . . When we consider what, to use the words of the catechism, is the chief end of man, and what are the true necessaries and means of life, it appears as if men had deliberately chosen the common mode of living because they preferred it to any other. Yet they honestly think there is no choice left. But alert and healthy natures remember that the sun rose clear. It is never too late to give up our prejudices.

WALDEN

## FEBRUARY 10

I trust that some may be as near and dear to Buddha, or Christ, or Swedenborg, who are without the pale of their churches. It is necessary not to be Christian to appreciate the beauty and significance of the life of Christ. I know that some will have hard thoughts of me, when they hear their Christ named beside my Buddha, yet I am sure that I am willing they should love their Christ more than my Buddha, for the love is the main thing, and I like him too. . . . Why need Christians be still intolerant and superstitious?

A WEEK ON THE CONCORD & MERRIMACK RIVERS

## FEBRUARY 11

By poverty, *i.e.* simplicity of life and fewness of incidents, I am solidified and crystallized, as a vapor or liquid by cold. It is a singular concentration of strength and energy and flavor. Chastity is perpetual acquaintance with the All. My diffuse and vaporous life becomes as the frost leaves and spiculae radiant as gems on the weeds and stubble in a winter morning. You think that I am impoverishing myself by withdrawing from men, but in my solitude I have woven for myself a silken web or *chrysalis*, and, nymph-like, shall ere long burst forth a more perfect creature, fitted for a higher society. By simplicity, commonly called poverty, my life is concentrated and so becomes organized, or a cosmos, which before was inorganic and lumpish.

JOURNAL 1857

## FEBRUARY 12

We cannot but pity the boy who has never fired a gun; he is no more humane, while his education has been sadly neglected. This was my answer with respect to the youths who were bent on this pursuit, trusting that they would soon outgrow it. No humane being, past the thoughtless age of boyhood, will wantonly murder any creature, which holds its life by the same tenure that he does. . . . Such is oftenest the young man's introduction to the forest, and the most original part of himself. He goes thither at first as a hunter and fisher, until at last, if he has the seeds of a better life in him, he distinguishes his proper objects, as a poet or naturalist it may be, and leaves the gun and fish-pole behind. . . . Thus, even in civilized communities, the embryo man passes through the hunter stage of development.

WALDEN

## FEBRUARY 13

I have met with but one or two persons in the course of my life who understood the art of Walking, that is, of taking walks, who had a genius, so to speak, for *sauntering*; which word is beautifully derived "from idle people who roved about the country, in the Middle Ages, and asked charity, under pretence of going *à la sainte terre*," to the holy land, till the children exclaimed, "There goes a *Sainte-Terrer*," a Saunterer, a Holy-Lander. They who never go to the Holy Land in their walks, as they pretend, are indeed mere idlers and vagabonds, but they who do go there are saunterers in the good sense, such as I mean. Some, however, would derive the word from *sans terre*, without land or a home, which, therefore, in the good sense, will mean, having no particular home, but equally at home everywhere. For this is the secret of successful sauntering. He who sits still in a house all the time may be the greatest vagrant of all, but the Saunterer, in the good sense, is no more vagrant than the meandering river, which is all the while sedulously seeking the shortest course to the sea. But I prefer the first, which indeed is the most probable derivation. For every walk is a sort of crusade, preached by some Peter the Hermit in us, to go forth and reconquer this Holy Land from the hands of the Infidels.

WALKING

## FEBRUARY 14

We boast that we belong to the nineteenth century and are making the most rapid strides of any nation. But consider how little this village does for its own culture.... We have a comparatively decent system of common schools,

schools for infants only. . . . It is time that we had uncommon schools, that we did not leave off our education when we begin to be men and women. It is time that villages were universities, and their elder inhabitants the fellows of universities, with leisure—if they are indeed so well off— to pursue liberal studies the rest of their lives. . . . To act collectively is according to the spirit of our institutions; and I am confident that, as our circumstances are more flourishing, our means are greater than the nobleman's. New England can hire all the wise men in the world to come and teach her, and board them round the while, and not be provincial at all. That is the *uncommon* school we want. Instead of noblemen, let us have noble villages of men. If it is necessary, omit one bridge over the river, go round a little there, and throw one arch at least over the darker gulf of ignorance which surrounds us.

WALDEN

## FEBRUARY 15

There is elevation in every hour. No part of the earth is so low and withdrawn that the heavens cannot be seen from it, but every part supports the sky. We have only to stand on the eminence of the hour, and look out thence into the empyrean, allowing no pinnacle above us, to command an uninterrupted horizon. The moments will lie outspread around us like a blue expanse of mountain and valley, while we stand on the summit of our hour as if we had descended on eagle's wings. For the eagle has stooped to his perch on the highest cliff and has never climbed the rock; he stands by his wings more than by his feet. We shall not want a foothold, but wings will sprout from our shoulders, and we shall walk securely, self-sustained.

## FEBRUARY 16

The commonest and cheapest sounds, as the barking of a dog, produce the same effect on fresh and healthy ears that the rarest music does. It depends on your appetite for sound. . . . It is better that these cheap sounds be music to us than that we have the rarest ears for music in any other sense. I have lain awake at night many a time to think of the barking of a dog which I had heard long before, bathing my being again in those waves of sound, as a frequenter of the opera might lie awake remembering the music he had heard.

## FEBRUARY 17

How prompt we are to satisfy the hunger and thirst of our bodies; how slow to satisfy the hunger and thirst of our *souls.* Indeed we who would be practical folks cannot use this word without blushing because of our infidelity, having starved this substance almost to a shadow. We feel it to be as absurd as if a man were to break forth into a eulogy on *his dog* who hasn't any. An ordinary man will work every day for a year at shovelling dirt to

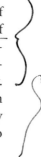

support his body, or a family of bodies, but he is an extraordinary man who will work a whole day in the year for the support of his soul. Even the priests, the men of God, so called, for the most part confess that they work for the support of the body. But he alone is the truly enterprising and practical man who succeeds in *maintaining* his soul here. Have we our everlasting life to get? And isn't that the only excuse at last for eating drinking sleeping or even carrying an umbrella when it rains?

LETTERS 1853

## FEBRUARY 18

For my part, I feel, that with regard to Nature, I live a sort of border life, on the confines of a world, into which I make occasional and transient forays only, and my patriotism and allegiance to the state into whose territories I seem to retreat are those of a moss-trooper. Unto a life which I call natural I would gladly follow even a will o' the-wisp through bogs and sloughs unimaginable, but no moon nor fire-fly has shown me the cause-way to it. Nature is a personality so vast and universal that we have never seen one of her features. The Walker in the familiar fields which stretch around my native town, sometimes finds himself in another land than is described in their owners' deeds, as it were in some far-away field on the confines of the actual Concord, where her jurisdiction ceases, and the idea which the word Concord suggests ceases to be suggested. These farms which I have myself surveyed, these bounds which I have set up appear dimly still as through a mist; but they have no chemistry to fix them; they fade from the surface of the glass; and the picture which the painter painted stands out dimly from beneath. The world with which we are commonly acquainted leaves no trace, and it will have no anniversary.

WALKING

## FEBRUARY 19

For many years I was self-appointed inspector of snow storms and rain storms, and did my duty faithfully; surveyor, if not of highways then of forest paths and all across-lot routes, keeping them open, and ravines bridged and passable at all seasons, where the public heel had testified to their utility. . . . Finding that my fellow-citizens were not likely to offer me any room in the court house, or any curacy or living any where else, but I must shift for myself, I turned my face more exclusively than ever to the woods, where I was better known. I determined to go into business at once, and not wait to acquire the usual capital, using such slender means as I had already got. My purpose in going to Walden Pond was not to live cheaply nor to live dearly there, but to transact some private business with the fewest obstacles; to be hindered from accomplishing which for want of a little common sense, a little enterprise and business talent, appeared not so sad as foolish.

WALDEN

## FEBRUARY 20

When I am going out for an evening I arrange the fire in my stove so that I do not fail to find a good one when I return, though it would have engaged my frequent attention present. So that, when I know I am to be at home, I sometimes make believe that I may go out, to save trouble. And this is the art of living, too,—to leave our life in a condition to go alone, and not to require a constant supervision. We will then sit down serenely to live, as by the side of a stove.

JOURNAL 1841

## FEBRUARY 21

It is easier to discover another such a new world as Columbus did, than to go within one fold of this which we appear to know so well; the land is lost sight of, the compass varies, and mankind mutiny; and still history accumulates like rubbish before the portals of nature. But there is only necessary a moment's sanity and sound senses, to teach us that there is a nature behind the ordinary, in which we have only some vague pre-emption right and western reserve as yet. We live on the outskirts of that region. Carved wood, and floating boughs, and sunset skies, are all that we know of it. We are not to be imposed on by the longest spell of weather. Let us not, my friends, be wheedled and cheated into good behavior to earn the salt of our eternal porridge, whoever they are that attempt it. Let us wait a little, and not purchase any clearing here, trusting that richer bottoms will soon be put up. It is but thin soil where we stand; I have felt my roots in a richer ere this.

A WEEK ON THE CONCORD & MERRIMACK RIVERS

## FEBRUARY 22

The whole of the day should not be daytime, nor of the night nighttime, but some portion be rescued from time to oversee time in. All our hours must not be current; all our time must not lapse. There must be one hour at least which the day did not bring forth,—of ancient parentage and long-established nobility,—which will be a serene and lofty platform overlooking the rest. We should make our notch every day on our characters, as Robinson Crusoe on his stick. We must be at the helm at least once a day; we must feel the tiller-rope in our hands, and know that if we sail, we steer.

JOURNAL 1841

## FEBRUARY 23

Our hymn-books resound with a melodious cursing of God and enduring Him forever. One would say that even the prophets and redeemers had rather consoled the fears than confirmed the hopes of man. There is nowhere recorded a simple and irrepressible satisfaction with the gift of life, any memorable praise of God. All health and success does me good, however far off and withdrawn it may appear; all disease and failure helps to make me sad and does me evil, however much sympathy it may have with me or I with it. If, then, we would indeed restore mankind by truly Indian, botanic, magnetic, or natural means, let us first be as simple and well as Nature ourselves, dispel the clouds which hang over our own brows, and take up a little life into our pores. Do not stay to be an overseer of the poor, but endeavor to become one of the worthies of the world.

WALDEN

## FEBRUARY 24

The higher the mountain on which you stand, the less change in the prospect from year to year, from age to age. Above a certain height, there is no change. . . . I have had but one *spiritual* birth (excuse the word), and now whether it rains or snows, whether I laugh or cry, fall farther below or approach nearer to my standard, whether Pierce or Scott is elected,—not a new scintillation of light flashes on me, but ever and anon, though with longer intervals, the same surprising and everlastingly new light dawns to me, with only such variations as in the coming of the natural day, with which, indeed, it is often coincident. As to how to preserve potatoes from rotting, your opinion may change from year to year, but as to how to preserve your soul from rotting, I have nothing to learn, but something to practice.

LETTERS 1853

## FEBRUARY 25

In the morning I bathe my intellect in the stupendous and cosmogonal philosophy of the Bhagvat Geeta, since whose composition years of the gods have elapsed, and in comparison with which our modern world and its literature seem puny and trivial; and I doubt if that philosophy is not to be referred to a previous state of existence, so remote is its sublimity from our conceptions. I lay down the book and go to my well for water, and lo! there I meet the servant of the Bramin, priest of Brahma and Vishnu and Indra, who sits in his temple on the Ganges reading the Vedas, or dwells at the root of a tree with his crust and water jug. I meet his servant come to draw water for his master, and our buckets as it were grate together in the same well. The pure Walden water is mingled with the sacred water of the Ganges.

WALDEN

## FEBRUARY 26

Above all, we cannot afford not to live in the present. He is blessed over all mortals who loses no moment of the passing life in remembering the past. Unless our philosophy hears the cock crow in every barn-yard within our horizon, it is belated. That sound commonly reminds us that we are growing rusty and antique in our employments and habits of thought. His philosophy comes down to a more recent time than ours. There is something suggested by it is a newer testament,—the gospel according to this moment. He has not fallen astern; he has got up early, and kept up early, and to be where he is is to be in season, in the foremost rank of time. It is an expression of the health and soundness of Nature, a brag for all the world—healthiness as of a spring burst forth a new fountain of the Muses, to celebrate this last instant of time.

WALKING

## FEBRUARY 27

In society you will not find health, but in nature. Unless our feet at least stood in the midst of nature, all our faces would be pale and livid. Society is always diseased, and the best is the most so. There is no scent in it so wholesome as that of the pines, nor any fragrance so penetrating and restorative as the life-everlasting in high pastures. I would keep some book of natural history always by me as a sort of elixir, the reading of which should restore the tone of the system. To the sick, indeed, nature is sick, but to the well, a fountain of health. To him who contemplates a trait of natural beauty no harm nor disappointment can come. The doctrines of despair, of spiritual or political tyranny or servitude, were never taught by such as shared the serenity of nature.

NATURAL HISTORY OF MASSACHUSETTS

The farmer is endeavoring to solve the problem of a livelihood by a formula more complicated than the problem itself. To get his shoestrings he speculates in herds of cattle. With consummate skill he has set his trap with a hair spring to catch comfort and independence, and then, as he turned away, got his own leg into it. This is the reason he is poor; and for a similar reason we are all poor in respect to a thousand savage comforts, though surrounded by luxuries. . . . And when the farmer has got his house, he may not be the richer but the poorer for it, and it be the house that has got him. . . . Granted that the *majority* are able at last either to own or hire the modern house with all its improvements. While civilization has been improving our houses, it has not equally improved the men who are to inhabit them. It has created palaces, but it was not so easy to create noblemen and kings.

WALDEN

# MARCH

## MARCH 1

When a man is warmed by the several modes which I have described, what does he want next? Surely not more warmth of the same kind, as more and richer food, larger and more splendid houses, finer and more abundant clothing, more numerous incessant and hotter fires, and the like. When he has obtained those things which are necessary to life, there is another alternative than to obtain the superfluities; and that is, to adventure on life now, his vacation from humbler toil having commenced. The soil, it appears, is suited to the seed, for it has sent its radicle downward, and it may now send its shoot upward also with confidence. Why has man rooted himself thus firmly in the earth, but that he may rise in the same proportion into the heavens above?

WALDEN

## MARCH 2

In literature, it is only the wild that attracts us. Dullness is but another name for tameness. It is the uncivilized free and wild thinking in Hamlet and the Iliad, in all the scriptures and mythologies, not learned in the schools, that delights us. As the wild duck is more swift and beautiful than the tame, so is the wild—the mallard—thought, which 'mid falling dews wings its way above the fens. A truly good book is something as natural, and as unexpectedly and unaccountably fair and perfect, as a wild flower discovered on the prairies of the West, or in the jungles of the East. Genius is a light which makes the darkness visible, like the lightning's flash, which perchance shatters the temple of knowledge itself—and not a taper lighted at the hearth-stone of the race, which pales before the light of common day.

WALKING

## MARCH 3

Men sometimes speak as if the study of the classics would at length make way for more modern and practical studies; but the adventurous student will always study classics, in whatever language they may be written and however ancient they may be. For what are the classics but the noblest recorded thoughts of man? They are the only oracles which are not decayed, and there are such answers to the most modern inquiry in them as Delphi and Dodona never gave. We might as well omit to study Nature because she is old. To read well, that is, to read true books in a true spirit, is a noble exercise, and one that will task the reader more than any exercise which the customs of the day esteem. It requires a training such as the athletes underwent, the steady intention almost of the whole life to this object. Books must be read as deliberately and reservedly as they were written.

WALDEN

## MARCH 4

We can only live healthily the life the gods assign us. I must receive my life as passively as the willow leaf that flutters over the brook. I must not be for myself, but God's work, and that is always good. I will wait the breezes patiently, and grow as Nature shall determine. My fate cannot but be grand so. We may live the life of a plant or an animal, without living an animal life. This constant and universal content of the animal comes of resting quietly in God's palm. I feel as if I could at any time resign my life and the responsibility of living into God's hands, and become as innocent, free from care, as a plant or stone. . . . My life, my life! why will you linger? Are the years short and the months of no account? How often has long delay quenched my aspirations! Can God afford that I should forget him? Is he so indifferent to my career? Can heaven be postponed with no more ado? Why were my ears given to hear those everlasting strains which haunt my life, and yet to be prophaned much more by these perpetual dull sounds?

JOURNAL 1842

## MARCH 5

Not without a slight shudder at the danger, I often perceive how near I had come to admitting into my mind the details of some trivial affair,—the news of the street; and I am astonished to observe how willing men are to lumber their minds with such rubbish,—to permit idle rumors and incidents of the most insignificant kind to intrude on ground which should be sacred to thought. Shall the mind be a public arena, where the affairs of the street and the gossip of the tea-table chiefly are discussed? Or shall it be a quarter of heaven itself,—a hypaethral temple, consecrated to the service of the gods? I find it so difficult to dispose of the few facts which to me are significant, that I hesitate to burden my attention with those which are insignificant, which only a divine mind could illustrate. Such is, for the most part, the news in newspapers and conversation. It is important to preserve the mind's chastity in this respect.

LIFE WITHOUT PRINCIPLE

## MARCH 6

How can a man sit down and quietly pare his nails, while the earth goes gyrating ahead amid such a din of sphere music, whirling him along about her axis some twenty-four thousand miles between sun and sun, but mainly in a circle some two millions of miles actual progress? And then such a hurly-burly on the surface—wind always blowing—now a zephyr, now a hurricane—tides never idle, ever fluctuating—no rest for Niagara, but perpetual ran-tan on those limestone rocks—and then that summer simmering which our ears are used to, which would otherwise be christened confusion worse confounded, but is now ironically called "silence audible," and above all the incessant tinkering named "hum of industry," the hurrying to and fro and confused jabbering of men. Can man do less than get up and shake himself?

JOURNAL 1838

## MARCH 7

The mystery of the life of plants is kindred with that of our own lives, and the physiologist must not presume to explain their growth according to mechanical laws, or as he might explain some machinery of his own making. We must not expect to probe with our fingers the sanctuary of any life, whether animal or vegetable. If we do, we shall discover nothing but surface still. The ultimate expression or fruit of any created thing is a fine effluence which only the most ingenuous worshipper perceives at a reverent distance from its surface even. The cause and the effect are equally evanescent and intangible, and the former must be investigated in the same spirit and with the same reverence with which the latter is perceived. Science is often like the grub which, though it may have nestled in the germ of a fruit, has merely blighted or consumed it and never truly tasted it.

JOURNAL 1859

## MARCH 8

I who cannot stay in my chamber for a single day without acquiring some rust, and when sometimes I have stolen forth for a walk at the eleventh hour of four o'clock in the afternoon, too late to redeem the day, when the shades of night were already beginning to be mingled with the day-light—have felt as if I had committed some sin to be atoned for, I confess that I am astonished at the power of endurance—to say nothing of the moral insensibility of my neighbors who confine themselves to shops and offices the whole day for weeks and months, aye and years almost together.

WALKING

## MARCH 9

There was an artist in the city of Kouroo who was disposed to strive after perfection. One day it came into his mind to make a staff. Having considered that in an imperfect work time is an ingredient, but into a perfect work time does not enter, he said to himself, It shall be perfect in all respects, though I should do nothing else in my life.... His singleness of purpose and resolution, and his elevated piety, endowed him, without his knowledge, with perennial youth. As he made no compromise with Time, Time kept out of his way, and only sighed at a distance because he could not overcome him.... When the finishing stroke was put to his work, it suddenly expanded before the eyes of the astonished artist into the fairest of all the creations of Brahma. He had made a new system in making a staff, a world with full and fair proportions; in which though the old cities and dynasties had passed away, fairer and more glorious ones had taken their places. And now he saw by the heap of shavings still fresh at his feet, that, for him and his work, the former lapse of time had been an illusion. . . . The material was pure, and his art was pure; how could the result be other than wonderful?

## MARCH 10

If these fields and streams and woods, the phenomena of nature here, and the simple occupations of the inhabitants should cease to interest and inspire me, no culture or wealth would atone for the loss. I fear the dissipation that travelling, going into society, even the best, the enjoyment of intellectual luxuries, imply. If Paris is much in your mind, if it is more and more to you, Concord is less and less, and yet it would be a wretched bargain to accept the proudest Paris in exchange for my native village. At best, Paris could only be a school in which to learn to live here, a stepping-stone to Concord, a school in which to fit for this university. I wish to live ever as to derive my satisfactions and inspirations from the commonest events, every-day phenomena, so that what my senses hourly perceive, my daily walk, the conversation of my neighbors, may inspire me, and I may dream of no heaven but that which lies about me. A man may acquire a taste for wine or brandy, and so lose his love for water, but should we not pity him?

## MARCH 11

There is always some accident in the best things, whether thoughts or expressions or deeds. The memorable thought, the happy expression, the admirable deed are only partly ours. The thought came to us because we were in a fit mood; also we were unconscious and did not know that we had said or done a good thing. We must walk consciously only part way toward our goal, and then leap in the dark to our success. What we do best or most perfectly is what we have most thoroughly learned by the longest practice, and at length it falls from us without our notice, as a leaf from a tree. It is the *last* time we shall do it,—our unconscious leavings.

JOURNAL 1859

## MARCH 12

It is essential that a man confine himself to pursuits—a scholar, for instance, to studies—which lie next to and conduce to his life, which do not go against the grain, either of his will or of his imagination. . . . Some men endeavor to live a constrained life, to subject their whole lives to their wills, as he who said he would give a sign if he were conscious after his head was cut off,—but he gave no sign. Dwell as near as possible to the channel in which your life flows. A man may associate with such companions, he may pursue such employments, as will darken the day for him. Men choose darkness rather than light.

JOURNAL 1853

## MARCH 13

The sad memory of departed friends is soon incrusted over with sublime and pleasing thoughts, as their monuments are overgrown with moss. Nature doth thus kindly heal every wound. By the mediation of a thousand little mosses and fungi, the most unsightly objects become radiant of beauty. There seem to be two sides to this world, presented us at different times, as we see things in growth or dissolution, in life or death. For seen with the eye of a poet, as God sees them, all are alive and beautiful; but seen with the historical eye, or the eye of the memory, they are dead and offensive. If we see Nature as pausing, immediately all mortifies and decays; but seen as progressing, she is beautiful.

JOURNAL 1842

## MARCH 14

In every threat and in every compliment there was a blunder; for they thought that my chief desire was to stand the other side of that stone wall. I could not but smile to see how industriously they locked the door on my meditations, which followed them out again without let or hindrance, and *they* were really all that was dangerous. As they could not reach me, they had resolved to punish my body; just as boys, if they cannot come at some person against whom they have a spite, will abuse his dog. I saw that the State was half-witted, that it was timid as a lone woman with her silver spoons, and that it did not know its friends from its foes, and I lost all my remaining respect for it, and pitied it.

RESISTANCE TO CIVIL GOVERNMENT

## MARCH 15

My life partakes of infinity. The air is as deep as our natures. Is the drawing in of this vital air attended with no more glorious results than I witness? The air is a velvet cushion against which I press my ear. I go forth to make new demands on life. I wish to begin this summer well; to do something in it worthy of it and me; to transcend my daily routine and that of my townsmen; to have my immortality now, that it be in the *quality* of my daily life; to pay the greatest price, the greatest tax, of any man in Concord, and enjoy it the most!! I will give all I am for *my* nobility. I will pay all my days for my success. I pray that the life of this spring and summer may ever lie fair in my memory. May I dare as I have never done! May I persevere as I have never done! May I purify myself anew as with fire and water, soul and body! May my melody not be wanting to the season! May I gird myself to be a hunter of the beautiful, that naught escape me! May I attain to a youth never attained! I am eager to report the glory of the universe; may I be worthy to do it; to have got through with regarding human values, so as not to be distracted from regarding divine values. It is reasonable that a man should be something worthier at the end of the year than he was at the beginning.

JOURNAL 1852

I do believe that the outward and the inward life correspond; that if any should succeed to live a higher life, others would not know of it; that difference and distance are one. To set about living a true life is to go on a journey to a distant country, gradually to find ourselves surrounded by new scenes and men; and as long as the old are around me, I know that I am not in any true sense living a new or better life. The outward is only the outside of that which is within. Men are not concealed under habits, but are revealed by them; they are their true clothes. I care not how curious a reason they may give for their abiding by them. Circumstances are not rigid and unyielding, but our habits are rigid. We are apt to speak vaguely sometimes, as if a divine life were to be grafted on to or built over this present as a suitable foundation. This might do if we could so build over our old life as to exclude from it all the warmth of our affection, and addle it, as the thrush builds over the cuckoo's egg, and lays her own atop, and hatches that only; but the fact is, we—so thin is the partition—hatch them both, and the cuckoo's always by a day first, and that young bird crowds the young thrushes out of the nest. No. Destroy the cuckoo's egg, or build a new nest.

LETTERS 1848

## MARCH 17

I am conscious of having, in my sleep, transcended the limits of the individual, and made observations and carried on conversations which in my waking hours I can neither recall nor appreciate. As if in sleep our individual fell into the infinite mind, and at the moment of awakening we found ourselves on the confines of the latter. On awakening we resume our enterprise, take up our bodies and become limited mind again. We meet and converse with those bodies which we have previously animated. There is a moment in the dawn, when the darkness of the night is dissipated and before the exhalations of the day commence to rise, when we see things more truly than at any other time. The light is more trustworthy, since our senses are purer and the atmosphere is less gross. By afternoon all objects are seen in mirage.

JOURNAL 1852

## MARCH 18

I do believe in simplicity. It is astonishing as well as sad, how many trivial affairs even the wisest man thinks he must attend to in a day; how singular an affair he thinks he must omit. When the mathematician would solve a difficult problem, he first frees the equation of all encumbrances, and reduces it to its simplest terms. So simplify the problem of life, distinguish the necessary and the real. Probe the earth to see where your main roots run. I would stand upon facts. Why not see,—use our eyes? Do men know nothing? I know many men who, in common things, are not to be deceived; who trust no moonshine; who count their money correctly, and know how to invest it; who are said to be prudent and knowing, who yet will stand at a desk the greater part of their lives, as cashiers in banks, and glimmer and rust and finally go out there. If they *know* anything, what under the sun do they do that for? Do they know what *bread* is? or what it is for? Do they know what life is? If they *knew* something, the places which know them now would know them no more forever.

LETTERS 1848

## MARCH 19

What a consolation are the stars to man!—so high and out of his reach, as is his own destiny. I do not know but my life is fated to be thus low and grovelling always. I cannot discover its use even to myself. But it is permitted to see those stars in the sky equally useless, yet highest of all and deserving of a fair destiny. My fate is in some sense linked with that of the stars, and if they are to persevere to a great end, shall I die who could conjecture it? It surely is some encouragement to know that the stars are my fellow-creatures, for I do not suspect but they are reserved for a high destiny. Has not he who discovers and names a planet in the heavens as long a year as it? I do not fear that any misadventure will befall *them*. Shall I not be content to disappear with the missing stars? Do I mourn their fate? Man's moral nature is a riddle which only eternity can solve.

JOURNAL 1842

## MARCH 20

Talk about a revival of religion! and business men's prayer-meetings! with which all the country goes mad now! What if it were as true and wholesome a *revival* as the little fishes feel which come out of the sluggish waters and run up the brooks toward their sources? All Nature *revives* at this season. With her it is really *a new life*, but with these church-goers it is only a revival of religion or hypocrisy. They go downstream to still muddier waters. It cheers me more to behold the swarms of gnats which have revived in the spring sun. The fish lurks by the mouth of its native brook, watching its opportunity to dart up the stream by the cakes of ice. . . . No wonder we feel the spring influences. There is a motion in the very ground under our feet. Each rill is peopled with new life rushing up it. If a man do not revive with nature in the spring, how shall he revive when a white-collared priest prays for him?

JOURNAL 1858

## MARCH 21

Our whole life is startlingly moral. There is never an instant's truce between virtue and vice. Goodness is the only investment that never fails. In the music of the harp which trembles round the world it is the insisting on this which thrills us. The harp is the travelling patterer for the Universe's Insurance Company, recommending its laws, and our little goodness is all the assessment that we pay. Though the youth at last grows indifferent, the laws of the universe are not indifferent, but are forever on the side of the most sensitive. Listen to every zephyr for some reproof, for it is surely there, and he is unfortunate who does not hear it. We cannot touch a string or move a stop but the charming moral transfixes us. Many an irksome noise, go a long way off, is heard as music, a proud sweet satire on the meanness of our lives.

WALDEN

## MARCH 22

I am not without hope that we may, even here and now obtain some accurate information concerning that *other world* which the instinct of mankind has so long predicted. Indeed, all that we call science, as well as all that we call poetry, is a particle of such information, accurate as far as it goes, though it be but to the confines of the truth. If we can reason so accurately, and with such wonderful confirmation of our reasoning, respecting so-called material objects and events infinitely removed beyond the range of our natural vision, so that the mind hesitates to trust its calculations even when they are confirmed by observation, why may not our speculations penetrate as far into the immaterial starry system, of which the former is but the outward and visible type? Surely, we are provided with senses as well fitted to penetrate the spaces of the real, the substantial, the eternal, as these outward are to penetrate the material universe.

A WEEK ON THE CONCORD & MERRIMACK RIVERS

## MARCH 23

The love is faint-hearted and short-lived that is contented with the past history of its object. It does not prepare the soil to bear new crops lustier than the old. "I would I had leisure for these things," sighs the world. "When I have done my quilting and baking, then I will not be backward." Love never stands still, nor does its object. It is the revolving sun and the swelling bud. If I know what I love, it is because I *remember* it. Life is grand, and so are its environments of Past and Future. Would the face of nature be so serene and beautiful if man's destiny were not equally so? What am I good for now, who am still marching after high things, but to hear and tell the news, to bring wood and water, and count how many eggs the hens lay? In the meanwhile, I expect my life will begin. I will not aspire longer. I will see what it is I would be after. I will be unanimous.

JOURNAL 1842

## MARCH 24

This, our respectable daily life, in which the man of common sense, the Englishman of the world, stands so squarely, and on which our institutions are founded, is in fact the veriest illusion, and will vanish like the baseless fabric of a vision; but that faint glimmer of reality which sometimes illuminates the darkness of daylight for all men, reveals something more solid and enduring than adamant, which is in fact the cornerstone of the world.

LETTERS 1848

## MARCH 25

Near the end of March, 1845, I borrowed an axe and went down to the woods by Walden Pond, nearest to where I intended to build my house, and began to cut down some tall, arrowy white pines, still in their youth, for timber. . . . They were pleasant spring days, in which the winter of man's discontent was thawing as well as the earth, and the life that had lain torpid began to stretch itself. One day, when my axe had come off and I had cut a green hickory for a wedge, driving it with a stone, and had placed the whole to soak in a pond-hole in order to swell the wood, I saw a striped snake run into the water, and he lay on the bottom, apparently without inconvenience, as long as I stayed there, or more than a quarter of an hour; perhaps because he had not yet fairly come out of the torpid state. It appeared to me that for a like reason men remain in their present low and primitive condition; but if they should feel the influence of the spring of springs arousing them, they would of necessity rise to a higher and more ethereal life.

WALDEN

## MARCH 26

The reading which I love best is the scriptures of the several nations, though it happens that I am better acquainted with those of the Hindoos, the Chinese, and the Persians, than of the Hebrews, which I have come to last. Give me one of these Bibles and you have silenced me for a while. When I recover the use of my tongue, I am wont to worry my neighbors with the new sentences; but commonly they cannot see that there is any wit in them.

A WEEK ON THE CONCORD & MERRIMACK RIVERS

## MARCH 27

Men cannot conceive of a state of things so fair that it cannot be realized. Can any man honestly consult his experience and say that it is so? Have we any facts to appeal to when we say that our dreams are premature? Did you ever hear of a man who had striven all his life faithfully and singly toward an object and in no measure obtained it? If a man constantly aspires, is he not elevated? Did ever a man try heroism, magnanimity, truth, sincerity, and find that there was no advantage in them? that it was a vain endeavor? Of course we do not expect that our paradise will be a garden. We know not what we ask. To look at literature;—how many fine thoughts has every man had! how few fine thoughts are expressed! Yet we never have a fantasy so subtle and ethereal, but that *talent merely*, with more resolution and faithful persistency, after a thousand failures, might fix and engrave it in distinct and enduring words, and we should see that our dreams are the solidest facts that we know. But I speak not of dreams. What can be expressed in words can be expressed in life.

LETTERS 1848

## MARCH 28

There is an incessant influx of novelty into the world, and yet we tolerate incredible dulness. I need only suggest what kind of sermons are still listened to in the most enlightened countries. There are such words as joy and sorrow, but they are only the burden of a psalm, sung with a nasal twang, while we believe in the ordinary and mean. We think that we can change our clothes only. . . . The life in us is like the water in the river. It may rise this year higher than man has ever known it, and flood the parched uplands; even this may be the eventful year, which will drown out all our muskrats. It was not always dry land where we dwell. I see far inland the banks which the stream anciently washed, before science began to record its freshets.

WALDEN

## MARCH 29

My actual life is a fact in view of which I have no occasion to congratulate myself; but for my faith and aspiration I have respect. It is from these that I speak. Every man's position is in fact too simple to be described. I have sworn no oath. I have no designs on society, or nature, or God. I am simply what I am, or I begin to be that. I *live* in the *present*. I only remember the past, and anticipate the future. I love to live. I love reform better than its modes. There is no history of how bad became better. I believe something, and there is nothing else but that. I know that I am. I know that another is who knows more than I, who takes interest in me, whose creature, and yet whose kindred, in one sense, am I. I know that the enterprise is worthy. I know that things work well. I have heard no bad news.

LETTERS 1848

## MARCH 30

Pursue, keep up with, circle round and round your life, as a dog does his master's chaise. Do what you love. Know your own bone; gnaw at it, bury it, unearth it, and gnaw it still. Do not be too moral. You may cheat yourself out of much life so. Aim above morality. Be not simply good; be good for something. All fables, indeed, have their morals; but the innocent enjoy the story. Let nothing come between you and the light. Respect men as brothers only. When you travel to the celestial city, carry no letter of introduction. When you knock ask to see God—none of the servants. In what concerns you much do not think that you have companions—know that you are alone in the world.

LETTERS 1848

One says to me, "I wonder that you do not lay up money; you love to travel; you might take the cars and go to Fitchburg to-day and see the country." But I am wiser than that. I have learned that the swiftest traveller is he that goes afoot. I say to my friend, Suppose we try who will get there first. The distance is thirty miles; the fare ninety cents. That is almost a day's wages. I remember when wages were sixty cents a day for laborers on this very road. Well, I start now on foot, and get there before night; I have travelled at that rate by the week together. You will in the meanwhile have earned your fare, and arrive there some time to-morrow, or possibly this evening, if you are lucky enough to get a job in season. Instead of going to Fitchburg, you will be working here the greater part of the day.

WALDEN

# APRIL

## APRIL 1

We have heard of a Society for the Diffusion of Useful Knowledge. It is said that Knowledge is power; and the like. Methinks there is equal need of a Society for the Diffusion of Useful Ignorance, what we will call Beautiful Knowledge, a knowledge useful in a higher sense; for what is most of our boasted so-called knowledge but a conceit that we know something, which robs us of the advantage of our actual ignorance? What we call knowledge is often our positive ignorance; ignorance our negative knowledge. By long years of patient industry and reading of the newspapers,—for what are the libraries of science but files of newspapers?—a man accumulates a myriad facts, lays them up in his memory, and then when in some spring of his life he saunters abroad into the Great Fields of thought, he as it were goes to grass like a horse, and leaves all his harness behind in the stable. I would say to the Society for the Diffusion of Useful Knowledge, sometimes—Go to grass. You have eaten hay long enough.

WALKING

## APRIL 2

I read in the Gulistan, or Flower Garden, of Sheik Sadi of Shiraz, that "they asked a wise man, saying: Of the many celebrated trees which the Most High God has created lofty and umbrageous, they call none azad, or free, excepting the cypress, which bears no fruit; what mystery is there in this? He replied: Each has its appropriate produce, and appointed season, during the continuance of which it is fresh and blooming, and during their absence dry and withered; to neither of which states is the cypress exposed, being always flourishing; and of this nature are the azads, or religious independents.— Fix not thy heart on that which is transitory; for the Dijlah, or Tigris, will continue to flow through Bagdad after the race of caliphs is extinct: if thy hand has plenty, be liberal as the date tree; but if it affords nothing to give away, be an azad, or free man, like the cypress."

WALDEN

## APRIL 3

Will you live? or will you be embalmed? Will you live, though it be astride of a sunbeam; or will you repose safely in the catacombs for a thousand years? . . . Men make a great ado about the folly of demanding too much of life (or of eternity?), and of endeavoring to live according to that demand. It is much ado about nothing. No harm ever came from that quarter. I am not afraid that I shall exaggerate the value and significance of life, but that I shall not be up to the occasion which it is. I shall be sorry to remember that I was there, but noticed nothing remarkable, not so much as a prince in disguise; lived in the golden age a hired man; visited Olympus even, but fell asleep after dinner, and did not hear the conversation of the gods. I lived in Judea eighteen hundred years ago, but I never knew that there was such a one as Christ among my contemporaries!

LETTERS 1850

## APRIL 4

The atmosphere of morning gives a healthy hue to our prospects. Disease is a sluggard that overtakes, never encounters, us. We have the start each day, and may fairly distance him before the dew is off; but if we recline in the bowers of noon, he will come up with us after all. The morning dew breeds no cold. We enjoy a diurnal reprieve in the beginning of each day's creation. In the morning we do not believe in expediency; we will start afresh, and have no patching, no temporary fixtures. The afternoon man has an interest in the past; his eye is divided, and he sees indifferently well either way. Drifting in a sultry day on the sluggish waters of the pond, I almost cease to live and begin to be. A boat-man stretched on the deck of his craft, and dallying with the noon, would be as apt an emblem of eternity for me as the serpent with his tail in his mouth. I am never so prone to lose my identity. I am dissolved in the haze.

JOURNAL 1839

## APRIL 5

Any prospect of awakening or coming to life to a dead man makes indifferent all times and places. The place where that may occur is always the same, and indescribably pleasant to all our senses. For the most part we allow only outlying and transient circumstances to make our occasions. They are, in fact, the cause of our distraction. Nearest to all things is that power which fashions their being. *Next* to us the grandest laws are continually being executed. *Next* to us is not the workman whom we have hired, with whom we love so well to talk, but the workman whose work we are.

WALDEN

## APRIL 6

It is true, we are but faint hearted crusaders, even the walkers, now-a-days, who undertake no persevering never ending enterprises. Our expeditions are but tours and come round again at evening to the old hearth side from which we set out. Half the walk is but retracing our steps. We should go forth on the shortest walk, perchance, in the spirit of undying adventure, never to return; prepared to send back our embalmed hearts only, as relics to our desolate kingdoms. If you are ready to leave father and mother, and brother and sister, and wife and child and friends, and never see them again; if you have paid your debts, and made your will, and settled all your affairs, and are a free man; then you are ready for a walk.

WALKING

## APRIL 7

As the truest society approaches always nearer to solitude, so the most excellent speech finally falls into
Silence. We go about to find Solitude and Silence, as
though they dwelt only in distant glens and the depth of
the wood, venturing out from these fortresses at midnight, and do not dream that she is then imported into
them when we wend thither. . . . Silence is the com-
muning of a conscious soul with itself. When we attend
for a moment to our own infinity, then and there is
silence, audible to all men at all times in all places. It is
when we hear inwardly; sound when we hear outwardly.

JOURNAL 1844


## APRIL 8

"That in which men differ from brute beasts," says
Mencius, "is a thing very inconsiderable; the common
herd lose it very soon; superior men preserve it careful-
ly." Who knows what sort of life would result if we had
attained to purity? If I knew so wise a man as could teach
me purity I would go to seek him forthwith. "A command over our passions, and over the external senses of
the body, and good acts, are declared by the Veda to be
indispensable in the mind's approximation to God." Yet
the spirit can for the time pervade and control every
member and function of the body, and transmute what
in form is the grossest sensuality into purity and devotion. The generative energy, which, when we are loose,

dissipates and makes us unclean, when we are continent invigorates and inspires us. Chastity is the flowering of man; and what are called Genius, Heroism, Holiness, and the like, are but various fruits which succeed it. Man flows at once to God when the channel of purity is open. By turns our purity inspires and our impurity casts us down. He is blessed who is assured that the animal is dying out in him day by day, and the divine being established. Perhaps there is none but has cause for shame on account of the inferior and brutish nature to which he is allied. I fear that we are such gods or demigods only as fauns and satyrs, the divine allied to beasts, the creatures of appetite, and that, to some extent, our very life is our disgrace.

WALDEN

## APRIL 9

Seen from a lower point of view, the Constitution, with all its faults, is very good; the law and the courts are very respectable; even this State and this American government are, in many respects, very admirable and rare things, to be thankful for, such as a great many have described them. . . . They who know of no purer sources of truth, who have traced up its stream no higher, stand, and wisely stand, by the Bible and the Constitution, and drink at it there with reverence and humility; but they who behold where it comes trickling into this lake or that pool, gird up their loins once more, and continue their pilgrimage toward its fountain-head.

RESISTANCE TO CIVIL GOVERNMENT

The morning, which is the most memorable season of the day, is the awakening hour. Then there is least somnolence in us; and for an hour, at least, some part of us awakes which slumbers all the rest of the day and night. Little is to be expected of that day, if it can be called a day, to which we are not awakened by our Genius, but by the mechanical nudgings of some servitor, are not awakened by our own newly-acquired force and aspirations from within, accompanied by the undulations of celestial music, instead of factory bells, and a fragrance filling the air—to a higher life than we fell asleep from; and thus the darkness bear its fruit, and prove itself to be good, no less than the light. That man who does not believe that each day contains an earlier, more sacred, and auroral hour than he has yet profaned, has despaired of life, and is pursuing a descending and darkening way. After a partial cessation of his sensuous life, the soul of man, or its organs rather, are reinvigorated each day, and his Genius tries again what noble life it can make. All memorable events, I should say, transpire in morning time and in a morning atmosphere.

WALDEN

## APRIL 11

In whatever moment we awake to life, as now I this evening after walking along the bank, and hearing the same evening sounds that were heard of yore it seems to have slumbered just below the surface, as in the spring the new verdure which covers the fields has never retreated far from the winter. All actions and objects and events lose their *distinct* importance in this hour, in the brightness of the vision, as, when sometimes the pure light that attends the setting sun falls on the trees and houses. The light itself is the phenomenon, and no single object is so distinct to our admiration as the light itself. For the most part we think there are but few degrees of sublimity, that the highest is but little higher than that we now behold. But we are always deceived—sublimer visions appear—and the former pale and fade away.

JOURNAL 1842

## APRIL 12

Let God alone if need be. Methinks, if I loved him more, I should keep him,—I should keep myself rather,—at a more respectful distance. It is not when I am going to meet him, but when I am just turning away and leaving him alone, that I discover that God is. I say, God. I am not sure that that is the name. You will know whom I mean. If for a moment we make way with our petty selves, wish no ill to anything, apprehend no ill, cease to be but as the crystal which reflects a ray,—what shall we not reflect! What a universe will appear crystallized and radiant around us!

LETTERS 1850

Thus it seemed that this one hillside illustrated the principle of all the operations of Nature. The Maker of this earth but patented a leaf. What Champollion will decipher this hieroglyphic for us, that we may turn over a new leaf at last? This phenomenon is more exhilarating to me than the luxuriance and fertility of vineyards. True, it is somewhat excrementitious in its character, and there is no end to the heaps of liver, lights, and bowels, as if the globe were turned wrong side outward; but this suggests at least that Nature has some bowels, and there again is mother of humanity. This is the frost coming out of the ground; this is Spring. . . . The earth is not a mere fragment of dead history, stratum upon stratum like the leaves of a book, to be studied by geologists and antiquaries chiefly, but living poetry like the leaves of a tree, which precede flowers and fruit,—not a fossil earth, but a living earth; compared with whose great central life all animal and vegetable life is merely parasitic.

WALDEN

We are accustomed to say in New England that few and fewer pigeons visit us every year. Our forests furnish no mast for them. So, it would seem, few and fewer thoughts visit each growing man from year to year, for the grove in our minds is laid waste,—sold to feed unnecessary fires of ambition, or sent to mill, and there is scarcely a twig left for them to perch on. They no longer build nor breed with us. In some more genial season, perchance, a faint shadow flits across the landscape of the mind, cast by the wings of some thought in its vernal or autumnal migration, but looking up, we are unable to detect the substance of the thought itself. Our winged thoughts are turned to poultry.

WALKING

## APRIL 15

I have travelled a good deal in Concord; and everywhere, in shops, and offices, and fields, the inhabitants have appeared to me to be doing penance in a thousand remarkable ways. What I have heard of Bramins sitting exposed to four fires and looking in the face of the sun; or hanging suspended, with their heads downward, over flames; or looking at the heavens over their shoulders "until it becomes impossible for them to resume their natural position, while from the twist of the neck nothing but liquids can pass into the stomach;" or dwelling, chained for life, at the foot of a tree; or measuring with their bodies, like caterpillars, the breadth of vast empires; or standing on one leg on the tops of pillars,— even these forms of conscious penance are hardly more incredible and astonishing than the scenes which I daily witness. The twelve labors of Hercules were trifling in comparison with those which my neighbors have undertaken; for they were only twelve, and had an end; but I could never see that these men slew or captured any monster or finished any labor.

WALDEN

## APRIL 16

We contemplated at our leisure the lapse of the river and of human life; and as that current, with its floating twigs and leaves, so did all things pass in review before us, while far away in cities and marts on this very stream, the old routine was proceeding still. There is, indeed, a tide in the affairs of men, as the poet says, and yet as things flow they circulate, and the ebb always balances the flow. All streams are but tributary to the ocean, which itself does not stream, and the shores are unchanged, but in longer periods than man can measure. Go where we will, we discover infinite change in particulars only, not in generals.

A WEEK ON THE CONCORD & MERRIMACK RIVERS

## APRIL 17

There is none who does not lie hourly in the respect he pays to false appearance. How sweet it would be to treat men and things, for an hour, for just what they are! We wonder that the sinner does not confess his sin. When we are weary with travel, we lay down our load and rest by the wayside. So, when we are weary with the burden of life, why do we not lay down this load of falsehoods which we have volunteered to sustain, and be refreshed as never mortal was? Let the beautiful laws prevail. Let us not weary ourselves by resisting them. When we would rest our bodies we cease to support them; we recline on the lap of earth. So, when we would rest our spirits, we must recline on the Great Spirit. Let things alone; let them weigh what they will; let them soar or fall. To succeed in letting only one thing alone in a winter morning, if it be only one poor frozen-thawed apple that hangs on a tree, what a glorious achievement! Methinks it lightens through the dusky universe. What an infinite wealth we have discovered! God reigns, *i.e.*, when we take a liberal view,—when a liberal view is presented us.

LETTERS 1850

## APRIL 18

What extracts from the Vedas I have read fall on me like the light of a higher and purer luminary, which describes a loftier course through a purer stratum,—free from particulars, simple, universal. It rises on me like the full moon after the stars have come out, wading through some far summer stratum of the sky. . . . I do not prefer one religion or philosophy to another. I have no sympathy with the bigotry and ignorance which make transient and partial and puerile distinctions between one man's faith or form of faith and another's—as Christian and heathen. I pray to be delivered from narrowness, partiality, exaggeration, bigotry. To the philosopher all sects, all nations, are alike. I like Brahma, Hare Buddha, the Great Spirit, as well as God.

JOURNAL 1850

## APRIL 19

To speak impartially, the best men that I know are not serene, a world in themselves. For the most part, they dwell in forms, and flatter and study effect only more finely than the rest. We select granite for the underpinning of our houses and barns; we build fences of stone; but we do not ourselves rest on an underpinning of granitic truth, the lowest primitive rock. Our sills are rotten. What stuff is the man made of who is not coexistent in our thought with the purest and subtilest truth? I often accuse my finest acquaintences of an immense frivolity; for, while there are manners and compliments we do not meet, we do not teach one another the lessons of honesty and sincerity that the brutes do, or of steadiness and solidity that the rocks do. The fault is commonly mutual, however; for we do not habitually demand any more of each other.

LIFE WITHOUT PRINCIPLE

## APRIL 20

Why level downward to our dullest perception always, and praise that as common sense? The commonest sense is the sense of men asleep, which they express by snoring. Sometimes we are inclined to class those who are once-and-a-half-witted with the half-witted, because we appreciate only a third part of their wit. Some would find fault with the morning red, if they ever got up early enough. "They pretend," as I hear, "that the verses of Kabir have four different senses; illusion, spirit, intellect, and the exoteric doctrine of the Vedas;" but in this part of the world it is considered a ground for complaint if a man's writings admit of more than one interpretation.

WALDEN

## APRIL 21

There are perturbations in our orbits produced by the influence of outlying spheres, and no astronomer has ever yet calculated the elements of that undiscovered world which produces them. I perceive in the common train of my thoughts a natural and uninterrupted sequence, each implying the next, or, if interruption occurs, it is occasioned by a new object being presented to my *senses*. But a steep, and sudden, and by these means unaccountable transition, is that from a comparatively narrow and partial, what is called common sense view of things, to an infinitely expanded and liberating one, from seeing things as men describe them, to seeing them as men cannot describe them. This implies a sense which is not common, but rare in the wisest man's experience; which is sensible or sentient of more than common.

A WEEK ON THE CONCORD & MERRIMACK RIVERS

## APRIL 22

Few phenomena gave me more delight than to observe the forms which thawing sand and clay assume in flowing down the sides of a deep cut on the railroad through which I passed on my way to the village. . . . What makes this sand foliage remarkable is its springing into existence thus suddenly. When I see on the one side the inert bank,—for the sun acts on one side first,—and on the other this luxuriant foliage, the creation of an hour, I am affected as if in a peculiar sense I stood in the laboratory of the Artist who made the world and me. . . . I feel as if I were nearer to the vitals of the globe, for this sandy overflow is something such a foliaceous mass as the vitals of the animal body. You thus find in the very sands an anticipation of the vegetable leaf. No wonder that the earth expresses itself outwardly in leaves, it so labors with the idea inwardly. The atoms have already learned this law and are pregnant by it. . . . What is man but a mass of thawing clay? The ball of the human finger is but a drop congealed. The fingers and toes flow to their extent from the thawing mass of the body. Who knows what the human body would expand and flow out to under a more genial heaven?

WALDEN

## APRIL 23

The West of which I speak is but another name for the Wild; and what I have been preparing to say is, that in

Wildness is the preservation of the world. Every tree sends its fibres forth in search of the Wild. The cities import it at any price. Men plow and sail for it. From the forest and wilderness come the tonics and barks which brace mankind. Our ancestors were savages. The story of Romulus and Remus being suckled by a wolf is not a meaningless fable. The founders of every state which has risen to eminence, have drawn their nourishment and vigor from a similar wild source. . . . I believe in the forest, and in the meadow, and in the night in which the corn grows. We require an infusion of hemlock spruce or Arbor vitae in our tea. . . . Give me a wildness whose glance no civilization can endure,—as if we lived on the marrow of koodoos devoured raw.

WALKING

## APRIL 24

There is a season for everything, and we do not notice a given phenomenon except at that season, if, indeed, it can be called the same phenomenon at any other season. There is a time to watch the ripples on Ripple Lake, to look for arrowheads, to study the rocks and lichens, a time to walk on sandy deserts; and the observer of nature must improve these seasons as much as the farmer his. So boys fly kites and play ball or hawkie at particular times all over the State. . . . We must not be governed by rigid rules, as by the almanac, but let the season rule us. The moods and thoughts of man are revolving just as steadily and incessantly as nature's. Nothing must be postponed. Take time by the forelock. Now or never! You must live in the present, launch yourself on every wave, find your eternity in each moment. Fools stand on their island opportunities and look toward another land. There is no other land; there is no other life but this, or the like of this. Where the good husbandman is, there is the good soil. Take any other course, and life will be a succession of regrets. Let us see vessels sailing prosperously before the wind, and not simply stranded barks. There is no world for the penitent and regretful.

JOURNAL 1859

## APRIL 25

Successive nations perchance have drunk at, admired, and fathomed it, and passed away, and still its water is green and pellucid as ever. Not an intermitting spring! Perhaps on that spring morning when Adam and Eve were driven out of Eden Walden Pond was already in existence, and even then breaking up in a gentle spring rain accompanied with mist and a southerly wind, and covered with myriads of ducks and geese, which had not heard of the fall, when still such pure lakes sufficed them. Even then it had commenced to rise and fall, and had clarified its waters and colored them of the hue they now wear, and obtained a patent of Heaven to be the only Walden Pond in the world and distiller of celestial dews. Who knows in how many unremembered nations' literatures this has been the Castalian Fountain? or what nymphs presided over it in the Golden Age? It is a gem of the first water which Concord wears in her coronet.

## APRIL 26

The charm of the Indian to me is that he stands free and unconstrained in Nature, is her inhabitant and not her guest, and wears her easily and gracefully. But the civilized man has the habits of the house. His house is a prison, in which he finds himself oppressed and confined, not sheltered and protected. He walks as if he sustained the roof; he carries his arms as if the walls would fall in and crush him, and his feet remember the cellar beneath. His muscles are never relaxed. It is rare that he overcomes the house, and learns to sit at home in it, and roof and floor and walls support themselves, as the sky and trees and earth. It is a great art to saunter.

## APRIL 27

I say, beware of all enterprises that require new clothes, and not rather a new wearer of clothes. If there is not a new man, how can the new clothes be made to fit? If you have any enterprise before you, try it in your old clothes. All men want, not something to *do with*, but something to *do*, or rather something to *be*. Perhaps we should never procure a new suit, however ragged or dirty the old, until we have so conducted, so enterprised or sailed in some way, that we feel like new men in the old. . . . We don garment after garment, as if we grew like exogenous plants by addition without. Our outside and often thin and fanciful clothes are our epidermis, or false skin, which partakes not of our life, and may be stripped off here and there without fatal injury.

WALDEN

## APRIL 28

There are old heads in the world who cannot help me by their example or advice to live worthily and satisfactorily to myself; but I believe that it is in my power to elevate myself this very hour above the common level of my life. It is better to have your head in the clouds, and know where you are, if indeed you cannot get it above them, than to breathe the clearer atmosphere below them, and think that you are in paradise.

LETTERS 1853

## APRIL 29

I have read in a Hindoo book, that "there was a king's son, who, being expelled in infancy from his native city, was brought up by a forester, and, growing up to maturity in that state imagined himself to belong to the barbarous race with which he lived. One of his father's ministers having discovered him, revealed to him what he was, and the misconception of his character was removed, and he knew himself to be a prince. So soul," continues the Hindoo philosopher, "from the circumstances in which it is placed, mistakes its own character, until the truth is revealed to it by some holy teacher, and then it knows itself to be Brahme." I perceive that we inhabitants of New England live this mean life that we do because our vision does not penetrate the surface of things. We think that that is which appears to be. If a man should walk through this town and see only the reality, where, think you, would the "Mill-dam" go to? If he should give us an account of the realities he beheld there, we should not recognize the place in his description.

WALDEN


## APRIL 30

Every one finds by his own experience, as well as in history, that the era in which men cultivate the apple, and the amenities of the garden, is essentially different from that of the hunter and forest life, and neither can displace the other without loss. We have all had our daydreams, as well as more prophetic nocturnal vision; but as for farming, I am convinced that my genius dates from an older era than the agricultural. . . . There is in my nature, methinks, a singular yearning toward all wildness. I know of no redeeming qualities in myself but a sincere love for some things, and when I am reproved I fall back on to this ground. What have I to do with ploughs? I cut another furrow than you see.

A WEEK ON THE CONCORD & MERRIMACK RIVERS

MAY

## MAY 1

It is foolish for a man to accumulate material wealth chiefly, houses and land. Our stock in life, our real estate, is that amount of thought which we have had, which we have thought out. The ground we have thus created is forever pasturage for our thoughts. I fall back on to visions which I have had. What else adds to my possessions and makes me rich in all lands? If you have ever done any work with these finest tools, the imagination and fancy and reason, it is a new creation, independent on the world, and a possession forever. You have laid up something against a rainy day. You have to that extent cleared the wilderness.

JOURNAL 1857

## MAY 2

If one hesitates in his path, let him not proceed. Let him respect his doubts, for doubts, too, may have some divinity in them. That we have but little faith is not sad, but that we have little faithfulness. By faithfulness faith is earned. When, in the progress of a life, a man swerves, though only by an angle infinitely small, from his proper and allotted path . . . then the drama of his life turns to tragedy, and makes haste to its fifth act. When once we thus fall behind ourselves, there is no accounting for the obstacles which rise up in our path, and no one is so wise as to advise, and no one so powerful as to aid us while we abide on that ground.

LETTERS 1848

## MAY 3

If you would learn to speak all tongues and conform to the customs of all nations, if you would travel farther than all travellers, be naturalized in all climes, and cause the Sphinx to dash her head against a stone, even obey the precept of the old philosopher, and Explore thyself. Herein are demanded the eye and the nerve. Only the defeated and deserters go to the wars, cowards that run away and enlist. Start now on that farthest western way, which does not pause at the Mississippi or the Pacific, nor conduct toward a worn-out China or Japan, but leads on direct, a tangent to this sphere, summer and winter, day and night, sun down, moon down, and at last earth down too.

WALDEN

## MAY 4

The fickle person is he that does not know what is true or right absolutely,—who has not an ancient wisdom for a lifetime, but a new prudence for every hour. We must sail by a sort of dead reckoning on this course of life, not speak any vessel nor spy any headland, but, in spite of all phenomena, come steadily to port at last. In general we must have a catholic and universal wisdom, wiser than any particular, and be prudent enough to defer to it always. We are literally wiser than we know. Men do not fail for want of knowledge, but for want of prudence to give wisdom the preference.

JOURNAL 1841

## MAY 5

You ask if there is no doctrine of sorrow in my philosophy. Of acute sorrow I suppose that I know comparatively little. My saddest and most genuine sorrows are apt to be but transient regrets. The place of sorrow is supplied, perchance, by a certain hard and proportionately barren indifference. I am of kin to the sod, and partake largely of its dull patience,—in winter expecting the sun of spring. In my cheapest moments I am apt to think that it isn't my business to be "seeking the spirit," but as much its business to be seeking me. I know very well what Goethe meant when he said that he never had a chagrin but he made a poem out of it. I have altogether too much patience of this kind. I am too easily contented with a slight and almost animal happiness. My happiness is a good deal like that of the woodchucks.

LETTERS 1848


## MAY 6

How important is a constant intercourse with nature and the contemplation of natural phenomena to the preservation of moral and intellectual health! The discipline of the schools or of business can never impart such serenity to the mind. The philosopher contemplates human affairs as calmly and from as great a remoteness as he does natural phenomena. The ethical philosopher needs the discipline of the natural philosopher. He approaches the study of mankind with great advantages who is accustomed to the study of nature.

JOURNAL 1851

## MAY 7

Men and boys are learning all kinds of trades but how to make *men* of themselves. They learn to make houses, but they are not so well housed, they are not so contented in their houses, as the woodchucks in their holes. What is the use of a house if you haven't got a tolerable planet to put it on?—if you cannot tolerate the planet it is on? Grade the ground first. If a man believes and expects great things of himself, it makes no odds where you put him, or what you show him, (of course, *you* cannot put him anywhere, nor show him anything), he will be surrounded by grandeur. He's in the condition of a healthy and hungry man, who says to himself, How sweet this crust is! If he despairs of himself, then Tophet is his dwelling-place, and he is in the condition of a sick man who is disgusted with the fruits of finest flavor.

LETTERS 1860

## MAY 8

At present, in this vicinity, the best part of the land is not private property; the landscape is not owned, and the walker enjoys comparative freedom. But possibly the day will come when it will be partitioned off into so-called pleasure grounds, in which a few will take a narrow and exclusive pleasure only,—when fences shall be multiplied, and man traps and other engines invented to confine men to the *public* road; and walking over the surface of God's earth, shall be construed to mean trespassing on some gentleman's grounds. To enjoy a thing exclusively is commonly to exclude yourself from the true enjoyment of it. Let us improve our opportunities then before the evil days come.

WALKING

## MAY 9

Whether he sleeps or wakes,—whether he runs or walks,—whether he uses a microscope or a telescope, or his naked eye, a man never discovers anything never overtakes anything, or leaves anything behind, but himself. Whatever he says or does he merely reports himself. If he is in love, he *loves*; if he is in heaven he *enjoys*; if he is in hell he *suffers*. It is his condition that determines his locality. The principal, the only thing a man makes, is his condition of fate. Though commonly he does not know it, nor put up a sign to this effect, "My own destiny made and mended here." (Not *yours*). He is a master-workman in this business. He works twenty-four hours a day at it, and gets it done. Whatever else he neglects or botches, no man was ever known to neglect this work. A great many pretend to make *shoes* chiefly, and would scout the idea that they make the hard times which they experience.

LETTERS 1860

## MAY 10

It is remarkable that, notwithstanding the universal favor with which the New Testament is outwardly received there is no appreciation of the order of truth with which it deals. There are, indeed, severe things in it which no man should read aloud more than once. "Seek first the kingdom of heaven." "Lay not up for yourselves treasures on earth." "If thou wilt be perfect, go and sell that thou hast, and give to the poor, and thou shalt have treasure in heaven." "For what is a man profited, if he shall gain the whole world, and lose his own soul? or what shall a man give in exchange for his soul?" Think of this, Yankees! "Verily, I say unto you, if ye have faith as a grain of mustard seed, ye shall say unto this mountain, Remove hence to yonder place; and it shall remove; and nothing shall be impossible unto you." Think of repeating these things to a New England audience! . . . Let but one of these sentences be rightly read, from any pulpit in the land, and there would not be left one stone of that meeting-house upon another.

A WEEK ON THE CONCORD & MERRIMACK RIVERS

## MAY 11

The thinker, he who is serene and self-possessed, is the brave, not the desperate soldier. He who can deal with his thoughts as a material, building them into poems in which future generations will delight, he is the man of the greatest and rarest vigor, not sturdy diggers and lusty polygamists. He is the man of energy, in whom subtle and poetic thoughts are bred. Common men can enjoy partially; they can go a-fishing rainy days; they can read poems perchance, but they have not the vigor to beget poems. They can enjoy feebly, but they cannot create. Men talk of freedom! How many are free to think? free from fear, from perturbation, from prejudice? Nine hundred and ninety-nine in a thousand are perfect slaves. How many can exercise the highest human faculties? He is the man truly—courageous, wise, ingenious—who can use his thoughts and ecstasies as the material of fair and durable creations. . . . The mass of men do not know how to cultivate the fields they traverse. The mass glean only a scanty pittance where the thinker reaps an abundant harvest. What is all your building, if you do not build with thoughts? No exercise implies more real manhood and vigor than joining thought to thought. How few men can tell what they have thought! I hardly know half a dozen who are not too lazy for this. They cannot get over some difficulty, and therefore they are on the long way round. You conquer fate by thought. . . . There is no more Herculean task than to think a thought about this life and then get it expressed.

JOURNAL 1858


## MAY 12

Where is the "Unexplored land" but in our own untried enterprises? To an adventurous spirit any place,— London, New York, Worcester, or his own yard, is "unexplored land," to seek which Freemont and Kane travel so far. To a sluggish and defeated spirit even the Great Basin and the Polaris are trivial places. If they can get there (and indeed they are there now), they will want to sleep, and give it up, just as they always do. These are the regions of the Known and of the Unknown. What is the use of going right over the old track again? There is an adder in the path which your own feet have worn. You must make tracks into the Unknown. That is what you have your board and clothes for. Why do you ever mend your clothes, unless that, wearing them, you may mend your ways? Let us sing.

LETTERS 1860

## MAY 13

Politics is, as it were, the gizzard of society, full of grit and gravel, and the two political parties are its opposite halves ... which grind on each other. Not only individuals, but states, have thus a confirmed dyspepsia, which expresses itself, you can imagine by what sort of eloquence. Thus our life is not altogether a forgetting, but also, alas! to a great extent, a remembering, of that which we should never have been conscious of, certainly not in our waking hours. Why should we not meet, not always as dyspeptics, to tell our bad dreams, but sometimes as *eu*peptics, to congratulate each other on the ever glorious morning? I do not make an exorbitant demand, surely.

LIFE WITHOUT PRINCIPLE

## MAY 14

We must learn to reawaken and keep ourselves awake, not by mechanical aids, but by an infinite expectation of the dawn, which does not forsake us in our soundest sleep. I know of no more encouraging fact than the unquestionable ability of man to elevate his life by a conscious endeavor. It is something to be able to paint a particular picture, or to carve a statue, and so to make a few objects beautiful; but it is far more glorious to carve and paint the very atmosphere and medium through which we look, which morally we can do. To affect the quality of the day, that is the highest of arts. Every man is tasked to make his life, even in its details, worthy of the contemplation of his most elevated and critical hour.

WALDEN

## MAY 15

As for the dispute about solitude and society, any comparison is impertinent. It is an idling down on the plain at the base of a mountain, instead of climbing steadily to its top. Of course you will be glad of all the society you can get to go up with. Will you go to glory with me? is the burden of the song. I love society so much that I swallowed it all at a gulp—that is, all that came in my way. It is not that we love to be alone, but that we love to soar, and when we do soar, the company grows thinner and thinner till there is none at all. It is either the *Tribune* on the plain, a sermon on the mount, or a very private ecstasy still higher up. We are not the less to aim at the summits, though the multitude does not ascend them. Use all the society that will abet you.

LETTERS 1856

## MAY 16

A written word is the choicest of relics. It is something at once more intimate with us and more universal than any other work of art. It is the work of art nearest to life itself. It may be translated into every language, and not only be read but actually breathed from all human lips;—not be represented on canvas or in marble only, but be carved out of the breath of life itself. The symbol of an ancient man's thought becomes a modern man's speech. Two thousand summers have imparted to the monuments of Grecian literature, as to her marbles, only a maturer golden and autumnal tint, for they have carried their own serene and celestial atmosphere into all lands to protect them against the corrosion of time. Books are the treasured wealth of the world and the fit inheritance of generations and nations. Books, the oldest and the best, stand naturally and rightfully on the shelves of every cottage. They have no cause of their own to plead, but while they enlighten and sustain the reader his common sense will not refuse them. Their authors are a natural and irresistible aristocracy in every society, and, more than kings or emperors, exert an influence on mankind.

WALDEN

It is remarkable that there is little or nothing to be remembered written on the subject of getting a living; how to make getting a living not merely honest and honorable, but altogether inviting and glorious; for if *getting* a living is not so, then living is not. One would think, from looking at literature, that this question had never disturbed a solitary individual's musings. Is it that men are too much disgusted with their experience to speak of it? The lesson of value which money teaches, which the Author of the Universe has taken so much pains to teach us, we are inclined to skip altogether. As for the means of living, it is wonderful how indifferent men of all classes are about it, even reformers, so called,—whether they inherit, or earn, or steal it. I think that Society has done nothing for us in this respect, or at least has undone what she has done. Cold and hunger seem more friendly to my nature than those methods which men have adopted and advise to ward them off.

LIFE WITHOUT PRINCIPLE

Men frequently say to me, "I should think you would feel lonesome down there, and want to be nearer to folks, rainy and snowy days and nights especially." I am tempted to reply to such—This whole earth which we inhabit is but a point in space. How far apart, think you, dwell the two most distant inhabitants of yonder star, the breadth of whose disk cannot be appreciated by our instruments? Why should I feel lonely? is not our planet in the Milky Way? This which you put seems to me not to be the most important question. What sort of space is that which separates a man from his fellows and makes him solitary? I have found that no exertion of the legs can bring two minds much nearer to one another. What do we want most to dwell near to? Not to many men surely, the depot, the post-office, the bar-room, the meeting-house, the school-house, the grocery, Beacon Hill, or the Five Points, where men most congregate, but to the perennial source of our life, whence in all our experience we have found that to issue, as the willow stands near the water and sends out its roots in that direction.

WALDEN

## MAY 19

If you take this life to be simply what old religious folks pretend, (I mean the effete, gone to seed in a drought, mere human galls stung by the devil once), then all your joy and serenity is reduced to grinning and bearing it. The fact is, you have got to take the world on your shoulders like Atlas and "put along" with it. You will do this for an idea's sake, and your success will be in proportion to your devotion to ideas. It may make your back ache occasionally, but you will have the satisfaction of hanging it or twirling it to suit yourself. Cowards suffer, heroes enjoy. After a long day's walk with it, pitch it into a hollow place, sit down and eat your luncheon. Unexpectedly, by some immortal thoughts, you will be compensated. The bank whereon you sit will be a fragrant and flowery one, and your world in the hollow a sleek and light gazelle.

LETTERS 1860

## MAY 20

There is, no doubt, a perfect analogy between the life of the human being and that of the vegetable, both of the body and the mind. . . . I am concerned first to come to my *Growth*, intellectually and morally (and physically, of course, as a means to this, for the body is the symbol of the soul), and then to bear my *Fruit*, do my *Work*, *propagate* my kind, not only physically but *morally*, not only in body but in mind. . . . So the mind develops from the first in two opposite directions: upwards to expand in the light and air; and downwards avoiding the light to form the root. One half is aërial, the other subterranean. The mind is not well balanced and firmly planted, like the oak, which has not as much root as branch, whose roots like those of the white pine are slight and near the surface. One half of the mind's development must still be root,—in the embryonic state, in the womb of nature, more unborn than at first. For each successive new idea or bud, a new rootlet in the earth. The growing man penetrates yet deeper by his roots into the womb of things. The infant is comparatively near the surface, just

covered from the light; but the man sends down a tap-root
to the centre of things.

## MAY 21

I do not mean to prescribe rules to strong and valiant
natures, who will mind their own affairs whether in
heaven or hell, and perchance build more magnificently
and spend more lavishly than the richest, without ever
impoverishing themselves. . . . I do not speak to those
who are well employed, in whatever circumstances, and
they know whether they are well employed or not;—but
mainly to the mass of men who are discontented, and
idly complaining of the hardness of their lot or of the
times, when they might improve them. There are some
who complain most energetically and inconsolably of
any, because they are, as they say, doing their duty. I also
have in my mind that seemingly wealthy, but most terri-
bly impoverished class of all, who have accumulated
dross, but know not how to use it, or get rid of it, and
thus have forged their own golden or silver fetters.

WALDEN

## MAY 22

I walk toward one of our ponds, but what signifies the
beauty of nature when men are base? We walk to lakes to
see our serenity reflected in them; when we are not
serene, we go not to them. Who can be serene in a coun-

try where both the rulers and the ruled are without principle? The remembrance of my country spoils my walk. My thoughts are murder to the State, and involuntarily go plotting against her. But it chanced the other day that I scented a white water-lily, and a season I had waited for had arrived. It is the emblem of purity. It bursts up so pure and fair to the eye, and so sweet to the scent, as if to show us what purity and sweetness reside in, and can be extracted from, the slime and muck of earth. I think I have plucked the first one that has opened for a mile. What confirmation of our hopes is in the fragrance of this flower! I shall not so soon despair of the world for it, notwithstanding slavery, and the cowardice and want of principle of Northern men. It suggests what kind of laws have prevailed longest and widest, and still prevail, and that the time may come when men's deeds will smell as sweet.

SLAVERY IN MASSACHUSETTS

## MAY 23

How shall we earn our bread is a grave question; yet it is a sweet and inviting question. Let us not shirk it, as is usually done. It is the most important and practical question which is put to man. Let us not answer it hastily. Let us not be content to get our bread in some gross, careless, and hasty manner. Some men go a-hunting, some a-fishing, some a-gaming, some to war; but none have so pleasant a time as they who in earnest seek to earn their bread. It is true actually as it is true really; it is true materially as it is true spiritually, that they who seek honestly and sincerely, with all their hearts and lives and strength, to earn their bread, do earn it, and it is sure to be very sweet to them. A very little bread,—a very few crumbs are enough, if it be of the right quality, for it is infinitely nutritious. Let each man, then, earn at least a crumb of bread for his body before he dies, and know the taste of it,—that it is identical with the bread of life, and that they both go down at one swallow.

LETTERS 1848

## MAY 24

Rather than love, than money, than fame, give me truth. I sat at a table where were rich food and wine in abundance, and obsequious attendance, but sincerity and truth were not; and I went away hungry from the inhospitable board. The hospitality was as cold as the ices. I thought that there was no need of ice to freeze them. They talked to me of the age of the wine and the fame of the vintage; but I thought of an older, a newer, and purer wine, of a more glorious vintage, which they had not got, and could not buy. The style, the house and grounds and "entertainment" pass for nothing with me. I called on the king, but he made me wait in his hall, and conducted like a man incapacitated for hospitality. There was a man in my neighborhood who lived in a hollow tree. His manners were truly regal. I should have done better had I called on him.

WALDEN

Our most glorious experiences are a kind of regret. Our regret is so sublime that we may take it for triumph. It is the painful, plaintively sad surprise of our Genius remembering our past lives and contemplating what is possible. It is remarkable that men commonly never refer to, never hint at, any crowning experiences when the common laws of their being were unsettled and the divine and eternal laws prevailed in them. Their lives are not revolutionary; they never recognize any other than the local and temporal authorities. It is a regret so divine and inspiring, so genuine, based on so true and distinct a contrast, that it surpasses our proudest boasts and the fairest expectations. My most sacred and memorable life is commonly on awakening in the morning. I frequently awake with an atmosphere about me as if my unremembered dreams had been divine, as if my spirit had journeyed to its native place, and, in the act of reentering its native body, had diffused an elysian fragrance around. The Genius says: "Ah! That is where you were! That is what you may yet be!" It is glorious for us to be able to regret even such an existence. A sane and growing man revolutionizes every day. What institutions of man can survive a morning experience? A single night's sleep, if we have indeed slumbered and forgotten anything and grown in our sleep, puts them behind us like the river Lethe. It is no unusual thing for him to see the kingdoms of this world pass away.

## MAY 26

I "never found any contentment in the life which the newspapers record"—any thing of more value than the cent which they cost. Contentment in being covered with dust an inch deep! We who walk the streets, and hold time together, are but the refuse of ourselves, and that life is for the shells of us,—of our body and our mind,—for our scurf,—a thoroughly *scurvy* life. It is coffee made of coffee-grounds the twentieth time, which was only coffee the first time,—while the living water leaps and sparkles by our doors. I know some who in their charity, give their coffee-grounds to the poor! We, demanding news, and putting up with *such* news! Is it a new convenience or a new accident, or, rather a new perception of the truth that we want?

LETTERS 1850

## MAY 27

But while we are confined to books, though the most select and classic, and read only particular written languages, which are themselves but dialects and provincial, we are in danger of forgetting the language which all things and events speak without metaphor, which alone is copious and standard. Much is published, but little printed. The rays which stream through the shutter will be no longer remembered when the shutter is wholly removed. No method nor discipline can supersede the necessity of being forever on the alert. What is a course of history, or philosophy, or poetry, no matter how well selected, or the best society, or the most admirable routine of life, compared with the discipline of looking always at what is to be seen? Will you be a reader, a student merely, or a seer? Read your fate, see what is before you, and walk on into futurity.

WALDEN

## MAY 28

The kings of England formerly had their forests "to hold the king's game," for sport or food, sometimes destroying villages to create or extend them; and I think that they were impelled by a true instinct. Why should not we, who have renounced the king's authority, have our national preserves, where no villages need be destroyed, in which the bear and panther, and some even of the hunter race, may still exist, and not be "civilized off the face of the earth,"—our forests, not to hold the king's game merely, but to hold and preserve the king himself also, the lord of creation,—not for idle sport or food, but for inspiration and our own true re-creation? or shall we, like villains, grub them all up, poaching on our own national domains?

THE MAINE WOODS

## MAY 29

If one listens to the faintest but constant suggestions of his genius, which are certainly true, he sees not to what extremes, or even insanity, it may lead him; and yet that way, as he grows more resolute and faithful, his road lies. The faintest assured objection which one healthy man feels will at length prevail over the arguments and customs of mankind. No man ever followed his genius till it misled him. Though the result were bodily weakness, yet perhaps no one can say that the consequences were to be regretted, for these were a life in conformity to higher principles. If the day and the night are such that you greet them with joy, and life emits a fragrance like flowers and sweet-scented herbs, is more elastic, more starry, more immortal,—that is your success. All nature is your congratulation, and you have cause momentarily to bless yourself. The greatest gains and values are farthest from being appreciated. We easily come to doubt if they exist. We soon forget them. They are the highest reality. Perhaps the facts most astounding and most real are never communicated by man to man. The true harvest of my daily life is somewhat as intangible and indescribable as the tints of morning or evening. It is a little star-dust caught, a segment of the rainbow which I have clutched.

WALDEN

## MAY 30

Some absorbing employment on your higher ground,— your upland farm,—whither no cartpath leads, but where you mount alone with your hoe,—where the life-everlasting grows; you raise a crop which needs not be brought down into the valley to a market; which you barter for heavenly products. Do you separate distinctly enough the support of your body from that of your essence? By how distinct a course commonly are these two ends attained! Not that they should not be attained by one and the same means—that indeed is the rarest success—but there is no half and half about it. . . . "Drink deep or taste not of the Pierian spring." Be not deterred by melancholy on the path which leads to immortal health and joy. When they tasted of the water of the river over which they were to go, they thought that tasted a little bitterish to the palate, but it proved sweeter when it was down.

LETTERS 1850

## MAY 31

Some incidents in my life have seemed far more allegorical than actual; they were so significant that they plainly served no other use. That is, I have been more impressed by their allegorical significance and fitness; they have been like myths or passages in a myth, rather than mere incidents or history which have to wait to become significant. Quite in harmony with my subjective philosophy. This, for instance: that, when I thought I knew the flowers so well, the beautiful purple azalea or pinxter-flower should be shown me by the hunter who found it. Such facts are lifted quite above the level of the actual. They are all just such events as my imagination prepares me for, no matter how incredible. Perfectly in keeping with my life and characteristic. Ever and anon something will occur which my philosophy has not dreamed of. The limits of the actual are set some thoughts further off. That which had seemed a rigid wall of vast thickness unexpectedly proves a thin and undulating drapery. The boundaries of the actual are no more fixed and rigid than the elasticity of our imaginations. The fact that a rare and beautiful flower which we never saw, perhaps never heard of, for which therefore there was no place in our thoughts, may at length be found in our immediate neighborhood, is very suggestive.

JOURNAL 1853

JUNE

## JUNE 1

Shams and delusions are esteemed for soundest truths, while reality is fabulous. If men would steadily observe realities only, and not allow themselves to be deluded, life, to compare it with such things as we know, would be like a fairy tale and the Arabian Nights' Entertainments. If we respected only what is inevitable and has a right to be, music and poetry would resound along the streets. When we are unhurried and wise, we perceive that only great and worthy things have any permanent and absolute existence,—that petty fears and petty pleasures are but the shadow of the reality. This is always exhilarating and sublime. By closing the eyes and slumbering, and consenting to be deceived by shows, men establish and confirm their daily life of routine and habit every where, which still is built on purely illusory foundations. Children, who play life, discern its true law and relations more clearly than men, who fail to live it worthily, but who think that they are wiser by experience, that is, by failure.

WALDEN

## JUNE 2

If I devote myself to other pursuits and contemplations, I must first see, at least, that I do not pursue them sitting upon another man's shoulders. I must get off him first, that he may pursue his contemplations too. See what gross inconsistency is tolerated. I have heard some of my townsmen say, "I should like to have them order me out to help put down an insurrection of the slaves, or to march to Mexico,—see if I would go"; and yet these very men have each, directly by their allegiance, and so indirectly, at least, by their money, furnished a substitute. The soldier is applauded who refuses to serve in an unjust war by those who do not refuse to sustain the unjust government which makes the war; is applauded by those whose own act and authority he disregards and sets at nought; as if the state were penitent to that degree that it hired one to scourge it while it sinned, but not to that degree that it left off sinning for a moment.

RESISTANCE TO CIVIL GOVERNMENT

## JUNE 3

There can be no very black melancholy to him who lives in the midst of Nature and has his senses still. There was never yet such a storm but it was Æolian music to a healthy and innocent ear. . . . While I enjoy the friendship of the seasons I trust that nothing can make life a burden to me. The gentle rain which waters my beans and keeps me in the house to-day is not drear and melancholy, but good for me too. . . . Sometimes, when I compare myself with other men, it seems as if I were more favored by the gods than they, beyond any deserts that I am conscious of; as if I had a warrant and surety at their hands which my fellows have not, and were especially guided and guarded. . . . I have never felt lonesome, or in the least oppressed by a sense of solitude, but once, and that was a few weeks after I came to the woods, when, for an hour, I doubted if the near neighborhood of man was not essential to a serene and healthy life. To be alone was something unpleasant. But I was at the same time conscious of a slight insanity in my mood, and seemed to foresee my recovery. In the midst of a gentle rain while these thoughts prevailed, I was suddenly sensible of such sweet and beneficent society in Nature, in the very pattering of the drops, and in every sound and sight around my house, an infinite and unaccountable friendliness all at once like an atmosphere sustaining me, as made the fancied advantages of human neighborhood insignificant, and I have never thought of them since.

WALDEN

## JUNE 4

I am convinced that there is no very important difference between a New-Englander's religion and a Roman's. We both worship in the shadow of our sins: they erect the temples for us. Jehovah has no superiority to Jupiter. The New-Englander is a pagan suckled in a creed outworn. Superstition has always reigned. It is absurd to think that these farmers, dressed in their Sunday clothes, proceeding to church, differ essentially in this respect from the Roman peasantry. They have merely changed the names and number of their gods. Men were as good then as they are now, and loved one another as much—or little.

JOURNAL 1853

## JUNE 5

It is so hard to forget what it is worse than useless to remember! If I am to be a thoroughfare, I prefer that it be of the mountain brooks, the Parnassian streams, and not the town sewers. There is inspiration, that gossip which comes to the ear of the attentive mind from the courts of heaven. There is the profane and stale revelation of the barroom and the police court. The same ear is fitted to receive both communications. Only the character of the hearer determines to which it shall be open, and to which closed. I believe that the mind can be permanently profaned by the habit of attending to trivial things, so that all our thoughts shall be tinged with triviality.

LIFE WITHOUT PRINCIPLE

## JUNE 6

But the walking of which I speak has nothing in it akin to taking exercise, as it is called, as the sick take medicine at stated hours—as the swinging of dumb-bells or chairs; but is itself the enterprise and adventure of the day. If you would get exercise go in search of the springs of life. Think of a man's swinging dumb-bells for his health, when those springs are bubbling up in far off pastures unsought by him. Moreover, you must walk like a camel which is said to be the only beast which ruminates when walking. When a traveller asked Wordsworth's servant to show him her master's study, she answered "Here is his library, but his study is out of doors."

## JUNE 7

We have wonderfully little faith. It seems so rare and dear, as if it were imported from very far. . . . Has man lived so long as to have learned the whole order of nature? Is it only the comets whose periods we have not wholly learned? What periods may love and justice have? What longer years revolve in the steady order of nature (whose spring our race never saw) quite distancing the memory of mankind, whose new spring may even now be at hand? Can our fathers tell us, even our forefathers, what we may expect in the future? What young experimentalists we are! There is not one here who has lived a whole human life, and can say what that is. As I stand today over the insect crawling amid the needles of the pine, and endeavoring to conceal himself from my sight and think what startling information I could give him concerning his fate and environments, I am led to ask if there may not be some infinite intelligence standing over me the human insect and preparing to impart to me knowledge as startling. Why will it cherish these humble thoughts and hide its head under the leaves to avoid his benefactor? I would cheer his puny race with fair news of great events which concern it. Might I not contribute something to strengthen its faith out of my superior

intelligence and make it bless that afternoon that led me
to the wood?

## JUNE 8

Practically, the old have no very important advice to give
the young, their own experience has been so partial, and
their lives have been such miserable failures, for private
reasons, as they must believe; and it may be that they
have some faith left which belies that experience, and
they are only less young than they were. I have lived
some thirty years on this planet, and I have yet to hear
the first syllable of valuable or even earnest advice from
my seniors. They have told me nothing, and probably
cannot tell me anything to the purpose. Here is life, an
experiment to a great extent untried by me; but it does
not avail me that they have tried it. If I have any experience which I think valuable, I am sure to reflect that this
my Mentors said nothing about.

## JUNE 9

There are as many strata at different levels of life as there
are leaves in a book. Most men probably have lived in
two or three. When on the higher levels we can remember the lower levels, but when when on the lower levels
we cannot remember the higher. My imagination, my
love and reverence and admiration, my sense of the

miraculous, is not so excited by any event as by the remembrance of my youth. Men talk about Bible miracles because there is no miracle in their lives. Cease to gnaw that crust. There is ripe fruit over your head. . . . We hug the earth. How rarely we mount! How rarely we climb a tree! We might get a little higher, methinks. That pine would make us dizzy. You can see the mountains from it as you never did before. Shall not a man have his spring as well as the plants?

JOURNAL 1850


## JUNE 10

Through our own recovered innocence we discern the innocence of our neighbors. You may have known your neighbor yesterday for a thief, a drunkard, or a sensualist, and merely pitied or despised him, and despaired of the world; but the sun shines bright and warm this first spring morning, re-creating the world, and you meet him at some serene work, and see how his exhausted and debauched veins expand with still joy and bless the new day, feel the spring influence with the innocence of infancy, and all his faults are forgotten. . . . Why the jailer does not leave open his prison doors,—why the judge does not dismiss his case,—why the preacher does not dismiss his congregation! It is because they do not obey the hint which God gives them, nor accept the pardon which he freely offers to all.

WALDEN

## JUNE 11

The woodland paths are never seen to such advantage as in a moonlight night, so embowered, still opening before you almost against expectation as you walk; you are so completely in the woods, and yet your feet meet no obstacles. It is as if it were not a path, but an open, winding passage through the bushes, which your feet find. Now I go by the spring, and when I have risen to the same level as before, find myself in the warm stratum again. The woods are about as destitute of inhabitants at night as the streets. In both there will be some night-walkers. There are but few wild creatures to seek their prey. The greater part of its inhabitants have retired to rest. Ah, that life that I have known! How hard it is to remember what is most memorable! We remember how we itched, not how our hearts beat. I can sometimes recall to mind the quality, the immortality, of my youthful life, but in memory is the only relation to it.

JOURNAL 1851


## JUNE 12

I am astonished at the singular pertinacity and endurance of our lives. The miracle is, that what is *is*, when it is so difficult, if not impossible, for anything else to be; that we walk on in our particular paths so far, before we fall on death and fate, merely because we must walk in some path; that every man can get a living, and so few can do anything more. So much only can I accomplish ere health and strength are gone, and yet this suffices. . . . I am never rich in money, and I am never meanly poor. If debts are incurred, why, debts are in the course of events cancelled, as it were by the same law by which they were incurred. . . . Our particular lives seem of such fortune and confident strength and durability as piers of solid rock thrown forward into the tide of circumstance. When every other path would fail, with singular and unerring confidence we advance on our particular course. What risks we run! famine and fire and pestilence, and the thousand forms of a cruel fate,— and yet every man lives till he—dies. How did he manage that? . . . My life will wait for nobody, but is being matured still without delay. . . . It will cut its own channel like a mountain stream, and by the longest ridge is not kept from the sea at last. I have found all things thus far, persons and inanimate matter, elements and seasons, strangely adapted to my resources.

A WEEK ON THE CONCORD & MERRIMACK RIVERS

## JUNE 13

We do not commonly live our life out and full; we do not fill all our pores with our blood; we do not inspire and expire fully and entirely enough, so that the wave, the comber, of each inspiration shall break upon our extremest shores, rolling till it meets the sand which bounds us, and the sound of the surf come back to us. Might not a bellows assist us to breathe? That our breathing should create a wind in a calm day! We live but a fraction of our life. Why do we not let on the flood, raise the gates, and set all our wheels in motion? He that hath ears to hear, let him hear. Employ your senses.

## JUNE 14

It struck me again to-night, as if I had not seen it almost daily for more than twenty years,—Why, here is Walden, the same woodland lake that I discovered so many years ago; where a forest was cut down last winter another is springing up by its shore as lustily as ever; the same thought is welling up to its surface that was then; it is the same liquid joy and happiness to itself and its Maker, ay, and it *may* be to me. It is the work of a brave man surely, in whom there was no guile! He rounded this water with his hand, deepened and clarified it in his thought, and in his will bequeathed it to Concord. I see by its face that it is visited by the same reflection; and I can almost say, Walden, is it you?

## JUNE 15

My friends wonder that I love to walk alone in solitary fields and woods by night. Sometimes in my loneliest and wildest moonlight walk I hear the sound of the whistle and the rattle of the cars, where perchance some of those very friends are being whirled by night over, as they think, a well-known, safe and public road. I see that men do not make or choose their own paths, whether they are railroads or trackless through the wilds, but what the powers permit each one enjoys. My solitary course has the same sanction that the Fitchburg Railroad has. If they have a charter from Massachusetts and—what is of much more importance—from Heaven, to travel the course and in the fashion they do, I have a charter, though it be from Heaven alone, to travel the course I do,—to take the necessary lands and pay the damages. It is by the grace of God in both cases.

JOURNAL 1850

## JUNE 16

The very simplicity and nakedness of man's life in the primitive ages imply this advantage at least, that they left him still but a sojourner in nature. When he was refreshed with food and sleep, he contemplated his journey again. He dwelt, as it were, in a tent in this world, and was either threading the valleys, or crossing the plains, or climbing the mountain-tops. But lo! men have become the tools of their tools. The man who independently plucked the fruits when he was hungry is become a farmer; and he who stood under a tree for shelter, a housekeeper. We now no longer camp as for a night, but have settled down on earth and forgotten heaven. We have adopted Christianity merely as an improved method of agri-culture. We have built for this world a family mansion, and for the next a family tomb. The best works of art are the expression of man's struggle to free himself from this condition, but the effect of our art is merely to make this low state comfortable and that higher state to be forgotten.

## JUNE 17

Where is the literature which gives expression to Nature? . . . I do not know of any poetry to quote which adequately expresses this yearning for the Wild. Approached from this side, the best poetry is tame. I do not know where to find in any literature, ancient or modern, any account which contents me of that Nature with which even I am acquainted. You will perceive that I demand something which no Augustan nor Elizabethan age, which no *culture*, in short, can give. Mythology comes nearer to it than anything. . . . Mythology is the crop which the Old World bore before its soil was exhausted, before the fancy and imagination were affected with blight; and which it still bears, wherever its pristine vigor is unabated.

## JUNE 18

The Vedas say, "All intelligences awake with the morning." Poetry and art, and the fairest and most memorable of the actions of men, date from such an hour. All poets and heroes, like Memnon, are the children of Aurora, and emit their music at sunrise. To him whose elastic and vigorous thought keeps pace with the sun, the day is a perpetual morning. It matters not what the clocks say or the attitudes and labors of men. Morning is when I am awake and there is a dawn in me. Moral reform is the effort to throw off sleep. Why is it that men give so poor an account of their day if they have not been slumbering? They are not such poor calculators. If they had not been overcome with drowsiness they would have performed something. The millions are awake enough for physical labor; but only one in a million is awake enough for effective intellectual exertion, only one in a hundred millions to a poetic or divine life. To be awake is to be alive. I have never yet met a man who was quite awake. How could I have looked him in the face?

WALDEN

## JUNE 19

I have a great deal of company in my house; especially in the morning, when nobody calls. Let me suggest a few comparisons, that some one may convey an idea of my situation. I am no more lonely than the loon in the pond that laughs so loud, or than Walden Pond itself. What company has that lonely lake, I pray? And yet it has not the blue devils, but the blue angels in it, in the azure tint of its waters. The sun is alone, except in thick weather, when there sometimes appear to be two, but one is a mock sun. God is alone,—but the devil, he is far from being alone; he sees a great deal of company; he is legion. I am no more lonely than a single mullein or dandelion in a pasture, or a bean leaf, or a sorrel, or a horse-fly, or a bumblebee. I am no more lonely than the Mill Brook, or a weathercock, or the north star, or the south wind, or an April shower, or a January thaw, or the first spider in a new house.

WALDEN

## JUNE 20

When the heavens are obscured to us, and nothing noble or heroic appears, but we are oppressed by imperfection and shortcoming on all hands, we are apt to suck our thumbs and decry our fates. As if nothing were to be done in cloudy weather, or, if heaven were not accessible by the upper road, men would not find out a lower. Sometimes I feel so cheap that I am inspired, and could write a poem about it,—but straight-way I cannot, for I am no longer mean. Let me know that I am ailing, and I am well. We should not always beat off the impression of trivialness, but make haste to welcome and cherish it. Water the weed till it blossoms; with cultivation it will bear fruit. There are two ways to victory,—to strive bravely, or to yield. How much pain the last will save us we have not yet learned.

JOURNAL 1840

## JUNE 21

If a man walk in the woods for love of them half of each day, he is in danger of being regarded as a loafer; but if he spends his whole day as a speculator, shearing off those woods and making the world bald before her time, he is esteemed an industrious and enterprising citizen. As if a town had no interest in its forests but to cut them down! Most men would feel insulted, if it were proposed to employ them in throwing stones over a wall, and then throwing them back, merely that they might earn their wages. But many are no more worthily employed now.

LIFE WITHOUT PRINCIPLE

## JUNE 22

I long for wildness, a nature which I cannot put my foot through, woods where the wood thrush forever sings, where the hours are early morning ones, and there is dew on the grass, and the day is forever unproved, where I might have a fertile unknown for a soil about me. I would go after the cows, I would watch the flocks of Admetus there forever, only for my board and clothes. A New Hampshire everlasting and unfallen. How wonderfully moral our whole life! There is never an instant's truce between virtue and vice. Goodness is the only investment that never fails. It is sung of in the music of the harp. . . . Though the youth at last grows indifferent, the laws of the universe are not indifferent; they are still and forever on the side of the most tender and sensitive.

JOURNAL 1853

## JUNE 23

As every season seems best to us in its turn, so the coming in of spring is like the creation of Cosmos out of Chaos and the realization of the Golden Age. . . . A single gentle rain makes the grass many shades greener. So our prospects brighten on the influx of better thoughts. We should be blessed if we lived in the present always, and took advantage of every accident that befell us, like the grass which confesses the influence of the slightest dew that falls on it; and did not spend our time in atoning for the neglect of past opportunities, which we call doing our duty. We loiter in winter while it is already spring. In a pleasant spring morning all men's sins are forgiven. Such a day is a truce to vice.

WALDEN

## JUNE 24

I am sane only when I have risen above my common sense, when I do not take the foolish view of things which is commonly taken, when I do not live for the low ends for which men commonly live. Wisdom is not common. To what purpose have I senses, if I am thus absorbed in affairs? My pulse must beat with Nature. After a hard day's work without a thought, turning my very brain into a mere tool, only in the quiet of evening do I so far recover my senses as to hear the cricket, which in fact has been chirping all day. In my better hours I am conscious of the influx of a serene and unquestionable wisdom which partly unfits, and if I yielded to it more rememberingly would wholly unfit me, for what is called the active business of life, for that furnishes nothing on which the eye of reason can rest. . . . Are our serene moments mere foretastes of heaven,—joys gratuitously vouchsafed to us as a consolation,—or simply a transient realization of what might be the whole tenor of our lives? . . . To be calm, to be serene! There is the calmness of the lake when there is not a breath of wind; there is the calmness of a stagnant ditch. So it is with us. Sometimes we are clarified and calmed healthily, as we never were before in our lives, not by an opiate, but by some unconscious obedience to the all—just laws, so that we become like a still lake of purest crystal and without an effort our depths are revealed to ourselves. All the world goes by us and is reflected in our deeps. Such clarity! obtained by such pure means! by simple living, by honesty of purpose. We live and rejoice. I awoke into a music which no one about me heard. Whom shall I thank for it? The luxury of wisdom! the luxury of virtue! Are there any intemperate in these things? I feel my Maker blessing me. To the sane man the world is a musical instrument. The very touch affords an exquisite pleasure.

JOURNAL 1851

## JUNE 25

Most people with whom I talk, men and women even of some originality and genius, have their scheme of the universe all cut and dried,—very *dry*, I assure you, to hear, dry enough to burn, dry-rotted and powder-post, methinks, which they set up between you and them in the shortest intercourse; an ancient and tottering frame with all its boards blown off. They do not walk without their bed. Some, to me, seemingly very unimportant and unsubstantial things and relations, are for them everlastingly settled,—as Father, Son, and Holy Ghost, and the like. These are like the everlasting hills to them. But in all my wanderings I never came across the least vestige of authority for these things. They have not left so distinct a trace as the delicate flower of a remote geological period on the coal in my grate.

A WEEK ON THE CONCORD & MERRIMACK RIVERS

## JUNE 26

However mean your life is, meet it and live it; do not shun it and call it hard names. It is not so bad as you are. It looks poorest when you are richest. The fault-finder will find faults even in paradise. Love your life, poor as it is. You may perhaps have some pleasant, thrilling, glorious hours, even in a poorhouse. The setting sun is reflected from the windows of the almshouse as brightly as from the rich man's abode; the snow melts before its door as early in the spring. I do not see but a quiet mind may live as contentedly there, and have as cheering thoughts, as in a palace. The town's poor seem to me often to live the most independent lives of any. . . . Cultivate poverty like a garden herb, like sage. Do not trouble yourself much to get new things, whether clothes or friends. Turn the old; return to them. Things do not change; we change. Sell your clothes and keep your thoughts. God will see that you do not want society.

WALDEN

## JUNE 27

Let men, true to their natures, cultivate the moral affections, lead manly and independent lives; let them make riches the means and not the end of existence, and we shall hear no more of the commercial spirit. The sea will not stagnate, the earth will be as green as ever, and the air as pure. This curious world which we inhabit is more wonderful than it is convenient, more beautiful than it is useful—it is more to be admired and enjoyed then, than used. The order of things should be somewhat reversed,—the seventh should be man's day of toil, wherein to earn his living by the sweat of his brow, and the other six his Sabbath of the affections and the soul, in which to range this wide-spread garden, and drink in the soft influences and sublime revelations of Nature.

THE COMMERCIAL SPIRIT

## JUNE 28

In my experience I have found nothing so truly impoverishing as what is called wealth, *i.e.*, the command of greater means than you had before possessed, though comparatively few and slight still, for you thus inevitably acquire a more expensive habit of living, and even the very same necessaries and comforts cost you more than they once did. Instead of gaining, you have lost some independence, and if your income should suddenly be lessened, you would find yourself poor, though possessed of the same means which once made you rich.

JOURNAL 1856

## JUNE 29

Some are dinning in our ears that we Americans, and moderns generally, are intellectual dwarfs compared with the ancients, or even the Elizabethan men. But what is that to the purpose? A living dog is better than a dead lion. Shall a man go and hang himself because he belongs to the race of pygmies, and not be the biggest pygmy that he can? Let every one mind his own business, and endeavor to be what he was made.

WALDEN

## JUNE 30

Farewell, my friends, my path inclines to this side the mountain, yours to that. For a long time you have appeared further and further off to me. I see that you will at length disappear altogether. For a season my path seems lonely without you. The meadows are like barren ground. The memory of me is steadily passing away from you. My path grows narrower and steeper, and the night is approaching. Yet I have faith that, in the definite future, new suns will rise, and new plains expand before me, and I trust that I shall therein encounter pilgrims who bear that same virtue that I recognized in you, who will be that very virtue that was you. I accept the ever-lasting and salutary law, which was promulgated as much that spring that I first knew you, as this that I seem to lose you.

JOURNAL 1856

JULY

## JULY 1

You can hardly convince a man of an error in a lifetime, but must content yourself with the reflection that the progress of science is slow. . . . I am not sure but I should betake myself in extremities to the liberal divinities of Greece, rather than to my country's God. Jehovah, though with us he has acquired new attributes, is more absolute and unapproachable, but hardly more divine, than Jove. He is not so much of a gentleman, not so gracious and catholic, he does not exert so intimate and genial an influence on nature, as many a god of the Greeks. . . . In my Pantheon, Pan still reigns in his pristine glory, with his ruddy face, his flowing beard, and his shaggy body, his pipe and his crook, his nymph Echo, and his chosen daughter Iambe; for the great god Pan is not dead, as was rumored. No god ever dies. Perhaps of all the gods of New England and of ancient Greece, I am most constant at his shrine.

A WEEK ON THE CONCORD & MERRIMACK RIVERS

## JULY 2

Most of the luxuries, and many of the so-called comforts of life, are not only not indispensable, but positive hindrances to the elevation of mankind. With respect to luxuries and comforts, the wisest have ever lived a more simple and meager life than the poor. The ancient philosophers, Chinese, Hindoo, Persian, and Greek, were a class than which none has been poorer in outward riches, none so rich in inward. We know not much about them. It is remarkable that we know so much of them as we do. The same is true of the more modern reformers and benefactors of their race. None can be an impartial or wise observer of human life but from the vantage ground of what we should call voluntary poverty. Of a life of luxury the fruit is luxury, whether in agriculture, or commerce, or literature, or art. There are nowadays professors of philosophy, but not philosophers. Yet it is admirable to profess because it was once admirable to live. To be a philosopher is not merely to have subtle thoughts, nor even to found a school, but so to love wisdom as to live according to its dictates, a life of simplicity, independence, magnanimity, and trust. It is to solve some of the problems of life, not only theoretically, but practically.

WALDEN

## JULY 3

Do we call this the land of the free? What is it to be free from King George and continue the slaves of King Prejudice? What is it to be born free and not to live free? What is the value of any political freedom, but as a means to moral freedom? Is it a freedom to be slaves, or a freedom to be free, of which we boast? We are a nation of politicians, concerned about the outmost defenses only of freedom. It is our children's children who may perchance be really free. We tax ourselves unjustly. There is a part of us which is not represented. It is taxation without representation. We quarter troops, we quarter fools and cattle of all sorts upon ourselves. We quarter our gross bodies on our poor souls, till the former eat up all the latter's substance.

LIFE WITHOUT PRINCIPLE

## JULY 4

When first I took up my abode in the woods, that is, began to spend my nights as well as days there, which, by accident, was on Independence Day, or the fourth of July, 1845, my house was not finished for winter, but was merely a defence against the rain, without plastering or chimney, the walls being of rough weather-stained boards, with wide chinks, which made it cool at night. The upright white hewn studs and freshly planed door and window casings gave it a clean and airy look, especially in the morning, when its timbers were saturated with dew, so that I fancied that by noon some sweet gum would exude from them. To my imagination it retained throughout the day more or less of this auroral character, reminding me of a certain house on a mountain which I had visited the year before. This was an airy and unplastered cabin, fit to entertain a travelling god, and where a goddess might trail her garments. The winds which passed over my dwelling were such as sweep over the ridges of mountains, bearing the broken strains, or celestial parts only, of terrestrial music. The morning wind forever blows, the poem of creation is uninterrupted; but few are the ears that hear it. Olympus is but the outside of the earth everywhere.

WALDEN

## JULY 5

This stray sound from a far-off sphere came to our ears from time to time, far, sweet, and significant, and we listened with such an unprejudiced sense as if for the first time we heard at all. No doubt he was an insignificant drummer enough, but his music afforded us a prime and leisure hour, and we felt that we were in season wholly. These simple sounds related to us the stars. Ay, there was a logic in them so convincing that the combined sense of mankind could never make me doubt their conclusions. I stop my habitual thinking, as if the plow had suddenly run deeper in its furrow through the crust of the world. How can I go on, who have just stepped over such a bottomless skylight in the bog of my life. Suddenly old Time winked at me,—Ah, you know me, you rogue,—and news had come that IT was well. That ancient universe is in such capital health, I think undoubtedly it will never die. Heal yourselves, doctors; by God I live. . . . I see, smell, taste, hear, feel, that everlasting Something to which we are allied, at once our maker, our abode, our destiny, our very Selves; the one historic truth, the most remarkable fact which can become the distinct and uninvited subject of our thought, the actual glory of the universe; the only fact which a human being cannot avoid recognizing, or in some way forget or dispense with. . . . I have seen how the foundations of the world are laid, and I have not the least doubt that it will stand a good while.

A WEEK ON THE CONCORD & MERRIMACK RIVERS

## JULY 6

There are a thousand hacking at the branches of evil to one who is striking at the root, and it may be that he who bestows the largest amount of time and money on the needy is doing the most by his mode of life to produce that misery which he strives in vain to relieve. . . . I would not subtract any thing from the praise that is due to philanthropy, but merely demand justice for all who by their lives and works are a blessing to mankind. I do not value chiefly a man's uprightness and benevolence, which are, as it were, his stem and leaves. . . . I want the flower and fruit of a man; that some fragrance be wafted over from him to me, and some ripeness flavor our intercourse. His goodness must not be a partial and transitory act, but a constant superfluity, which costs him nothing and of which he is unconscious.

WALDEN

## JULY 7

After reading Howitt's account of the Australian gold-diggings one evening . . . I was thinking, accidentally, of my own unsatisfactory life, doing as others do; and with that vision of the diggings still before me, I asked myself, why I might not be washing some gold daily, though it were only the finest particles,—why *I* might not sink a shaft down to the gold within me, and work that mine. *There* is a Ballarat, a Bendigo for you,—what though it were a sulky-gully? At any rate, I might pursue some path, however solitary and narrow and crooked, in which I could walk with love and reverence. Wherever a man separates from the multitude, and goes his own way in this mood, there indeed is a fork in the road, though ordinary travellers may see only a gap in the paling. His solitary path across lots will turn out the *higher way* of the two.

LIFE WITHOUT PRINCIPLE

## JULY 8

If the tax-gatherer, or any other public officer, asks me, as one has done, "But what shall I do?" my answer is, "If you really wish to do any thing, resign your office." When the subject has refused allegiance, and the officer has resigned his office, then the revolution is accomplished. But even suppose blood should flow. Is there not a sort of blood shed when the conscience is wounded? Through this wound a man's real manhood and immortality flow out, and he bleeds to an everlasting death. I see this blood flowing now.

RESISTANCE TO CIVIL GOVERNMENT

I said to myself, I will not plant beans and corn with so much industry another summer, but such seeds, if the seed is not lost, as sincerity, truth, simplicity, faith, innocence, and the like, and see if they will not grow in this soil, even with less toil and manurance, and sustain me, for surely it has not been exhausted for these crops. Alas! I said this to myself; but now another summer is gone, and another, and another, and I am obliged to say to you, Reader, that the seeds which I planted, if indeed they *were* the seeds of those virtues, were wormeaten or had lost their vitality, and so did not come up. Commonly men will only be brave as their fathers were brave, or timid. This generation is very sure to plant corn and beans each new year precisely as the Indians did centuries ago and taught the first settlers to do, as if there were a fate in it. I saw an old man the other day, to my astonishment, making the holes with a hoe for the seventieth time at least, and not for himself to lie down in! But why should not the New Englander try new adventures, and not lay so much stress on his grain, his potato and grass crop, and his orchards—raise other crops than these? Why concern ourselves so much about our beans for seed, and not be concerned at all about a new generation of men?

WALDEN

## JULY 10

My vicinity affords many good walks; and though for so many years I have walked almost every day, and sometimes for several days together, I have not yet exhausted them. An absolutely new prospect is a great happiness, and I can still get this any afternoon. Two or three hours' walking will carry me to as strange a country as I expect ever to see. A single farm-house which I had not seen before is sometimes as good as the dominions of the King of Dahomey. There is in fact a sort of harmony discoverable between the capabilities of the landscape within a circle of ten miles' radius, or the limits of an afternoon walk, and the threescore years and ten of human life. It will never become quite familiar to you.

WALKING

## JULY 11

What is called genius is the abundance of life or health, so that whatever addresses the senses, as the flavor of these berries, or the lowing of that cow, which sounds as if it echoed along a cool mountain-side just before night, where odoriferous dews perfume the air and there is everlasting vigor, serenity, and expectation of perpetual untarnished morning,—each sight and sound and scent and flavor,—intoxicates with a healthy intoxication. The shrunken stream of life overflows its banks, makes and fertilizes broad intervals from which generations derive their sustenances. This is the true overflowing of the

Nile. So exquisitely sensitive are we, it makes us embrace our fates, and, instead of suffering or indifference, we enjoy and bless. If we have not dissipated the vital, the divine, fluids, there is, then, a circulation of vitality beyond our bodies.

JOURNAL 1852

## JULY 12

Our life is frittered away by detail. An honest man has hardly need to count more than his ten fingers, or in extreme cases he may add his ten toes, and lump the rest. Simplicity, simplicity, simplicity! I say, let your affairs be as two or three, and not a hundred or a thousand; instead of a million count half a dozen, and keep your accounts on your thumb nail. In the midst of this chopping sea of civilized life, such are the clouds and storms and quick-sands and thousand-and-one items to be allowed for, that a man has to live, if he would not founder and go to the bottom and not make his port at all, by dead reckoning, and he must be a great calculator indeed who succeeds. Simplify, simplify. Instead of three meals a day, if it be necessary eat but one; instead of a hundred dishes, five; and reduce other things in proportion.

WALDEN

## JULY 13

Great God, I ask thee for no meaner pelf
Than that I may not disappoint myself,

That in my action I may soar as high,
As I can now discern with this clear eye.

And next in value, which thy kindness lends,
That I may greatly disappoint my friends,
Howe'er they think or hope that it may be,
They may not dream how thou'st distinguished me.

That my weak hand may equal my firm faith,
And my life practice more than my tongue saith;
That my low conduct may not show,
Nor my relenting lines,
That I thy purpose did not know,
Or overrated thy designs.

THE DIAL

## JULY 14

The youth gets together his materials to build a bridge to the moon, or perchance a palace or temple on earth, and at length the middle-aged man concludes to build a wood-shed with them. Trees commonly have two growths in the year, a spring and a fall growth, the latter sometimes equalling the former, and you can see where the first was checked whether by cold or drouth, and wonder what there was in the summer to produce this check, this blight. So is it with man; most have a spring growth only, and never get over this first check to their youthful hopes; but plants of hardier constitution, or perchance planted in a more genial soil, speedily recover themselves, and, though they bear the scar or knot in remembrance of their disappointment, they push forward again and have a vigorous fall growth which is equivalent to a new spring.

## JULY 15

How many a man has dated a new era in his life from the reading of a book! The book exists for us, perchance, which will explain our miracles and reveal new ones. The at present unutterable things we may find somewhere uttered. These same questions that disturb and puzzle and confound us have in their turn occurred to all the wise men; not one has been omitted; and each has answered them, according to his ability, by his words and his life. Moreover, with wisdom we shall learn liberality. The solitary hired man on a farm in the outskirts of Concord, who has had his second birth and peculiar religious experience, and is driven as he believes into silent gravity and exclusiveness by his faith, may think it is not true; but Zoroaster, thousands of years ago, travelled the same road and had the same experience; but he, being wise, knew it to be universal, and treated his neighbors accordingly, and is even said to have invented and established worship among men. Let him humbly commune with Zoroaster then, and, through the liberalizing influence of all the worthies, with Jesus Christ himself, and let "our church" go by the board.

I think that no experience which I have to-day comes up to, or is comparable with, the experiences of my boyhood. And not only this is true, but as far back as I can remember I have unconsciously referred to the experiences of a previous state of existence. . . . Formerly, methought, nature developed as I developed, and grew up with me. My life was ecstasy. In youth, before I lost any of my senses, I can remember that I was all alive, and inhabited my body with inexpressible satisfaction; both its weariness and its refreshment were sweet to me. This earth was the most glorious musical instrument, and I was audience to its strains. To have such sweet impressions made on us, such ecstasies begotten of the breezes! I can remember how I was astonished. I said to myself. . . . "There comes into my mind such indescribable, infinite, all-absorbing, divine, heavenly pleasure, a sense of elevation and expansion and I have had naught to do with it. I perceive that I am dealt with by superior powers. This is a pleasure, a joy, an existence which I have not procured myself. I speak as a witness on the stand, and tell what I have perceived." The morning and the evening were sweet to me, and I led a life aloof from society of men. I wondered if a mortal ever knew what I knew. I looked in books for some recognition of a kindred experience, but, strange to say, I found none. Indeed, I was slow to discover that other men had this experience. . . . The maker of me was improving me. When I detected this interference I was profoundly moved. For years I marched to a music in comparison with which the military music of the streets is noise and discord. I was daily intoxicated, and yet no man could call me intemperate. With all your science can you tell how it is, and whence it is, that light comes into the soul?

JOURNAL 1851

## JULY 17

Society is commonly too cheap. We meet at very short intervals, not having had time to acquire any new value for each other. We meet at meals three times a day, and give each other a new taste of that old musty cheese that we are. We have had to agree on a certain set of rules, called etiquette and politeness, to make this frequent meeting tolerable and that we need not come to open war. We meet at the post-office, and at the sociable, and about the fireside every night; we live thick and are in each other's way, and stumble over one another, and I think that we thus lose some respect for one another. Certainly less frequency would suffice for all important and hearty communications. Consider the girls in a factory,—never alone, hardly in their dreams. It would be better if there were but one inhabitant to a square mile, as where I live. The value of a man is not in his skin, that we should touch him.

WALDEN

## JULY 18

It is a test question affecting the youth of a person,—
Have you knowledge of the morning? Do you sympa-
thize with that season of nature? Are you abroad early,
brushing the dews aside? If the sun rises on you slumbering, if you do not hear the morning cock-crow, if you
do not witness the blushes of Aurora, if you are not
acquainted with Venus as the morning star, what relation have you to wisdom and purity? You have then forgotten your Creator in the days of your youth! Your
shutters were darkened till noon! You rose with a sick
headache! In the morning sing, as do the birds.

JOURNAL 1851

## JULY 19

When I would recreate myself, I seek the darkest wood,
the thickest and most interminable, and, to the citizen,
most dismal swamp. I enter a swamp as a sacred place—
a *sanctum sanctorum*. There is the strength—the marrow
of Nature. The wild wood covers the virgin mould, and
the same soil is good for men and for trees. A man's
health requires as many acres of meadow to his prospect
as his farm does loads of muck. There are the strong
meats on which he feeds. A town is saved, not more by
the righteous men in it, than by the woods and swamps
that surround it. A township where one primitive forest
waves above, while another primitive forest rots below—
such a town is fitted to raise not only corn and potatoes,

but poets and philosophers for the coming ages. In such a soil grew Homer and Confucius and the rest, and out of such a wilderness comes the reformer eating locusts and wild honey.

WALKING

## JULY 20

As I came home through the woods with my string of fish, trailing my pole, it being now quite dark, I caught a glimpse of a woodchuck stealing across my path, and felt a strange thrill of savage delight, and was strongly tempted to seize and devour him raw; not that I was hungry then, except for that wildness which he represented. Once or twice, however, while I lived at the pond, I found myself ranging the woods, like a half-starved hound, with a strange abandonment, seeking some kind of venison which I might devour, and no morsel could have been too savage for me. The wildest scenes had become unaccountably familiar. I found in myself, and still find, an instinct toward a higher, or, as it is named, spiritual life, as do most men, and another toward a primitive rank and savage one, and I reverence them both. I love the wild not less than the good.

WALDEN

## JULY 21

Now I yearn for one of those old, meandering, dry, uninhabited roads, which lead away from towns, which lead us away from temptation, which conduct to the outside of earth, over its uppermost crust; . . . along which you may travel like a pilgrim, going nowhither; where travellers are not too often to be met; where my spirit is free; where the walls and fences are not cared for; where your head is more in heaven than your feet are on earth; which have long reaches where you can see the approaching traveller half a mile off and be prepared for him; not so luxuriant a soil as to attract men; some root and stump fences which do not need attention; where travellers have no occasion to stop, but pass along and leave you to your thoughts; where it makes no odds which way you face, whether you are going or coming, whether it is morning or evening, mid-noon or midnight; where earth is cheap enough by being public; where you can walk and think with least obstruction, there being nothing to measure progress by; where you can pace when your breast is full, and cherish your moodiness; where you are not in false relations with men, are not dining nor conversing with them; by which you may go to the uttermost parts of the earth. . . . It must simply be the way and the life,—a way that was never known to be repaired, nor to need repair, within the memory of the oldest inhabitant.

JOURNAL 1851

## JULY 22

I have paid no poll-tax for six years. I was put into jail once on this account, for one night; and, as I stood considering the walls of solid stone, two or three feet thick, the door of wood and iron, a foot thick, and the iron grating which strained the light, I could not help being struck with the foolishness of that institution which treated me as if I were mere flesh and blood and bones, to be locked up. I wondered that it should have concluded at length that this was the best use it could put me to, and had never thought to avail itself of my services in some way. I saw that, if there was a wall of stone between me and my townsmen, there was a still more difficult one to climb or break through, before they could get to be as free as I was. I did not for a moment feel confined, and the walls seemed a great waste of stone and mortar. I felt as if I alone of all my townsmen had paid my tax.

RESISTANCE TO CIVIL GOVERNMENT

## JULY 23

Light-winged Smoke, Icarian bird,
Melting thy pinions in thy upward flight,
Lark without song, and messenger of dawn,
Circling above the hamlets as thy nest;
Or else, departing dream, and shadowy form
Of midnight vision, gathering up thy skirts;
By night star-veiling, and by day
Darkening the light and blotting out the sun;
Go thou my incense upward from this hearth,
And ask the gods to pardon this clear flame.

WALDEN

## JULY 24

Nature does her best to feed man. The traveller need not go out of the road to get as many as he wants; every bush and vine teems with palatable fruit. Man for once stands in such relation to Nature as the animals that pluck and eat as they do. The fields and hills are a table constantly spread. Wines of all kinds and qualities, of noblest vintage, are bottled up in the skins of countless berries, for the taste of men and animals. To men they seem offered not so much for food as for sociality, that they may picnic with Nature,—diet, drinks, cordials, wines. We pluck and eat in remembrance of Her. It is a sacrament, a communion. The not-forbidden fruits, which no serpent tempts us to taste.

JOURNAL 1853

## JULY 25

Why should we be in such desperate haste to succeed and in such desperate enterprises? If a man does not keep pace with his companions, perhaps it is because he hears a different drummer. Let him step to the music which he hears, however measured or far away. It is not important that he should mature as soon as an apple-tree or an oak. Shall he turn his spring into summer? If the condition of things which we were made for is not yet, what were any reality which we can substitute? We will not be shipwrecked on a vain reality. Shall we with pains erect a heaven of blue glass over ourselves, though when it is done we shall be sure to gaze still at the true ethereal heaven far above, as if the former were not?

WALDEN

## JULY 26

May I go to my slumbers as expecting to arise to a new and more perfect day. May I so live and refine my life as fitting myself for a society ever higher than I actually enjoy. May I treat myself tenderly as I would treat the most innocent child whom I love; may I treat children and my friends as my newly discovered self. Let me forever go in search of myself; never for a moment think that I have found myself; be as a stranger to myself, never a familiar, seeking acquaintance still. May I be to myself as one is to me whom I love, a dear and cherished object. What temple, what fane, what sacred place can there be but the innermost part of my own being? The possibility of my own improvement, that is to be cherished. As I regard myself, so I am. . . . I had ceased to have faith in myself. I thought I was grown up and become what I was intended to be, but it is earliest spring with me. In relation to virtue and innocence the oldest man is in the beginning spring and vernal season of life. It is the love of virtue makes us young ever. That is the fountain of youth, the very aspiration after the perfect. I love and worship myself with a love which absorbs my love for the world. . . . May I dream not that I shunned vice; may I dream that I loved and practiced virtue.

JOURNAL 1851

## JULY 27

Silence is audible to all men, at all times, and in all places. She is when we hear inwardly, sound when we hear outwardly. Creation has not displaced her, but is her visible framework and foil. All sounds are her servants, and purveyors, proclaiming not only that their mistress is, but is a rare mistress, and earnestly to be sought after. They are so far akin to Silence, that they are but bubbles on her surface, which straightway burst, an evidence of the strength and prolificness of the undercurrent; a faint utterance of Silence, and then only agreeable to our auditory nerves when they contrast themselves with and relieve the former. In proportion as they do this, and are heighteners and intensifiers of the Silence, they are harmony and purest melody.

A WEEK ON THE CONCORD & MERRIMACK RIVERS

## JULY 28

Here I am thirty-four years old, and yet my life is almost wholly unexpanded. How much is in the germ! There is such an interval between my ideal and the actual in many instances that I may say I am unborn. There is the instinct for society, but no society. Life is not long enough for one success. Within another thirty-four years that miracle can hardly take place. Methinks my seasons revolve more slowly than those of nature; I am differently timed. I am contented. This rapid revolution of nature, even of nature in me, why should it hurry me? Let a man step to the music which he hears, however measured. Is it important that I should mature as soon as an apple tree? aye, as soon as an oak? May not my life in nature, in proportion as it is supernatural, be only the spring and infantile portion of my spirit's life? Shall I turn my spring to summer? May I not sacrifice a hasty and petty completeness here to entireness there? If my curve is large, why bend it to a smaller circle? My spirit's unfolding observes not the pace of nature. The society which I was made for is not here. Shall I, then, substitute for the anticipation of that this poor reality? I would rather have the unmixed expectation of that than this reality. If life is a waiting, so be it. I will not be shipwrecked on a vain reality.

JOURNAL 1851

## JULY 29

This is a delicious evening, when the whole body is one sense, and imbibes delight through every pore. I go and come with a strange liberty in Nature, a part of herself. As I walk along the stony shore of the pond in my shirt sleeves, though it is cool as well as cloudy and windy, and I see nothing special to attract me, all the elements are unusually congenial to me. The bullfrogs trump to usher in the night, and the note of the whip-poor-will is borne on the rippling wind from over the water. Sympathy with the fluttering alder and poplar leaves almost takes away my breath; yet, like the lake, my serenity is rippled but not ruffled. These small waves raised by the evening wind are as remote from storm as the smooth reflecting surface. Though it is now dark, the wind still blows and roars in the wood, the waves still dash, and some creatures lull the rest with their notes. The repose is never complete. The wildest animals do not repose, but seek their prey now; the fox, and skunk, and rabbit, now roam the fields and woods without fear. They are Nature's watchmen,—links which connect the days of animated life.

WALDEN

## JULY 30

There is something servile in the habit of seeking after a law which we may obey. We may study the laws of matter at and for our convenience, but a successful life knows no law. It is an unfortunate discovery certainly, that of a law which binds us where we did not know before that we were bound. Live free, child of the mist— and with respect to knowledge we are all children of the mist. The man who takes the liberty to live is superior to all the laws both of heaven and earth, by virtue of his relation to the law-maker. "That is active duty," says the Vishnu Purana, "which is not for our bondage; that is knowledge which is for our liberation; all other duty is good only unto weariness; all other knowledge is only the cleverness of an artist."

WALKING

Be resolutely and faithfully what you are; be humbly what you aspire to be. Be sure you give men the best of your wares, though they be poor enough, and the gods will help you lay up a better store for the future. Man's noblest gift to man is his sincerity, for it embraces his integrity also. Let him not dole out of himself anxiously, to suit their weaker or stronger stomachs, but make a clean gift of himself, and empty his coffers at once. I would be in society as in the landscape; in the presence of nature there is no reserve, nor effrontery.

JOURNAL 1841

# AUGUST

## AUGUST 1

To the sick the doctors wisely recommend a change of air and scenery. Thank Heaven, here is not all the world. The buck-eye does not grow in New England, and the mocking-bird is rarely heard here. The wild-goose is more of a cosmopolite than we; he breaks his fast in Canada, takes a luncheon in the Ohio, and plumes himself for the night in a southern bayou. Even the bison, to some extent, keeps pace with the seasons, cropping the pastures of the Colorado only till a greener and sweeter grass awaits him by the Yellowstone. Yet we think that if rail-fences are pulled down, and stone-walls piled up on our farms, bounds are henceforth set to our lives and our fates decided. If you are chosen town clerk, forsooth, you cannot go to Tierra del Fuego this summer; but you may go to the land of infernal fire nevertheless. The universe is wider than our views of it.

WALDEN

## AUGUST 2

As for conforming outwardly, and living your own life inwardly, I do not think much of that. Let not your right hand know what your left hand does in that line of business. It will prove a failure. Just as successfully can you walk against a sharp steel edge which divides you cleanly right and left. Do you wish to try your ability to resist distension? It is a greater strain than any soul can long endure. When you get God to pulling one way and the devil the other, each having his feet well braced,—to say nothing of the conscience sawing transversely,—almost any timber will give way.

LETTERS 1850

## AUGUST 3

A thrumming of piano-strings beyond the gardens and through the elms. At length the melody steals into my being. I know not when it began to occupy me. By some fortunate coincidence of thought or circumstance I am attuned to the universe, I am fitted to hear, my being moves in a sphere of melody, my fancy and imagination are excited to an inconceivable degree. This is no longer the dull earth on which I stood. It is possible to live a grander life here; already the steed is stamping, the knights are prancing; already our thoughts bid a proud farewell to the so-called actual life and its humble glories. Now this is the verdict of a soul in health. But the soul diseased says that its own vision and life alone is true and sane. What a different aspect will courage put upon the face of things! This suggests what a perpetual flow of spirit would produce.

JOURNAL 1852

## AUGUST 4

We are for the most part more lonely when we go abroad among men than when we stay in our chambers. A man thinking or working is always alone, let him be where he will. Solitude is not measured by the miles of space that intervene between a man and his fellows. The really diligent student in one of the crowded hives of Cambridge College is as solitary as a dervish in the desert. The farmer can work alone in the field or the woods all day, hoeing or chopping, and not feel lonesome, because he is employed; but when he comes home at night he cannot sit down in a room alone, at the mercy of his thoughts, but must be where he can "see the folks," and recreate, and as he thinks remunerate himself for his day's solitude; and hence he wonders how the student can sit alone in the house all night and most of the day without ennui and "the blues"; but he does not realize that the student, though in the house, is still at work in *his* field, and chopping in *his* woods, as the farmer in his, and in turn seeks the same recreation and society that the latter does, though it may be a more condensed form of it.

WALDEN

## AUGUST 5

Was ever any virtue attributed to a man without exaggeration? was ever any vice, without infinite exaggeration? Do we not exaggerate ourselves to ourselves, or do we often recognize ourselves for the actual men we are? Are we not all great men? Yet what are we actually, to speak of? We live by exaggeration, what else is it to anticipate more than we enjoy? The lightening is an exaggeration of the light. Exaggerated history is poetry, and truth referred to a new standard. To a small man every greater is an exaggeration. He who cannot exaggerate is not qualified to utter truth. No truth we think was ever expressed but with this sort of emphasis, so that for the time there seemed to be no other. Moreover, you must speak loud to those who are hard of hearing, and so you acquire a habit of speaking loud to those who are not. By an immense exaggeration we appreciate our Greek poetry and philosophy, and Egyptian ruins; our Shakespeares and Miltons, our Liberty and Christianity. We give importance to this hour over all other hours. We do not live by justice, but by grace.

THOMAS CARLYLE AND HIS WORKS

## AUGUST 6

As I was leaving the Irishman's roof over the rain, bending my steps again to the pond, my haste to catch pickerel, wading in retired meadows, in sloughs and bog-holes, in forlorn and savage places, appeared for an instant trivial to me who had been sent to school and college; but as I ran down the hill toward the reddening west, with the rainbow over my shoulder, and some faint tinkling sounds borne to my ear through the cleansed air, from I know not what quarter, my Good Genius seemed to say,—Go fish and hunt far and wide day by day,—farther and wider,—and rest thee by many brooks and hearth-sides without misgiving. Remember thy Creator in the days of thy youth. Rise free from care before the dawn, and seek adventures. Let the noon find thee by other lakes, and the night overtake thee everywhere at home. There are no larger fields than these, no worthier games than may here be played. Grow wild according to thy nature, like these sedges and brakes, which will never become English hay. Let the thunder rumble; what if it threaten ruin to farmers' crops? That is not its errand to thee. Take shelter under the cloud, while they flee to carts and sheds. Let not to get a living be thy trade, but thy sport. Enjoy the land, but own it not. Through want of enterprise and faith men are where they are, buying and selling, and spending their lives like serfs.

WALDEN

## AUGUST 7

I rejoice that horses and steers have to be broken before they can be made the slaves of men, and that men themselves have some wild oats still left to sow before they become submissive members of society. Undoubtedly, all men are not equally fit subjects for civilization; and because the majority, like dogs and sheep, are tame by inherited disposition, is no reason why the others should have their natures broken that they may be reduced to the same level. Men are in the main alike, but they were made several in order that they might be various. If a low use is to be served, one man will do nearly or quite as well as another; if a high one, individual excellence is to be regarded.

WALKING

## AUGUST 8

The entertaining a single thought of a certain elevation makes all men of one religion. It is always some base alloy that creates the distinction of sects. Thought greets thought over the widest gulfs of time with unerring freemasonry. I know, for instance, that Sadi entertained once identically the same thought that I do, and thereafter I can find no essential difference between Sadi and myself. He is not Persian, he is not ancient, he is not strange to me. By the identity of his thoughts with mine he still survives. It makes no odds what atoms serve us. . . . I only know myself as a human entity, the scene, so to speak, of thoughts and affections, and am sensible of a certain doubleness by which I can stand as remote from myself as from another. However intense my experience, I am conscious of the presence and criticism of a part of me which, as it were, is not a part of me, but spectator, sharing no experience, but taking note of it, and that is no more I than it is you.

JOURNAL 1852

## AUGUST 9

If the injustice is part of the necessary friction of the machine of government, let it go, let it go; perchance it will wear smooth—certainly the machine will wear out. If the injustice has a spring, or a pulley, or a rope, or a crank, exclusively for itself, then perhaps you may consider whether the remedy will not be worse than the evil; but if it is of such a nature that it requires you to be the agent of injustice to another, then, I say, break the law. Let your life be a counter friction to stop the machine. What I have to do is to see, at any rate, that I do not lend myself to the wrong which I condemn.

RESISTANCE TO CIVIL GOVERNMENT

## AUGUST 10

How meanly and miserably we live for the most part! We escape fate continually by the skin of our teeth, as the saying is. We are practically desperate. But as every man, in respect to material wealth, aims to become independent or wealthy, so, in respect to our spirits and imagination, we should have some spare capital and superfluous vigor, have some margin and leeway in which to move. What kind of gift is life unless we have spirits to enjoy it and taste its true flavor? if, in respect to spirits, we are to be forever cramped and in debt? In our ordinary estate we have not, so to speak, quite enough air to breathe, and this poverty qualifies our piety; but we should have more than enough and breathe it carelessly. Poverty is the rule. We should first of all be full of vigor like a strong horse, and beside have the free and adventurous spirit of his driver; *i.e.*, we should have such a reserve of elasticity and strength that we may at any time be able to put ourselves at the top of our speed and go beyond our ordinary limits, just as the invalid hires a horse. Have the gods sent us into this world,—to this *muster*,—to do chores, hold horses, and the like, and not given us any spending money?

JOURNAL 1857

## AUGUST 11

I learned this, at least, by my experiment: that if one advances confidently in the direction of his dreams, and endeavors to live the life which he has imagined, he will meet with a success unexpected in common hours. He will put some things behind, will pass an invisible boundary; new, universal, and more liberal laws will begin to establish themselves around and within him; or the old laws be expanded, and interpreted in his favor in a more liberal sense, and he will live with the license of a higher order of beings. In proportion as he simplifies his life, the laws of the universe will appear less complex, and solitude will not be solitude, nor poverty poverty, nor weakness weakness. If you have built castles in the air, your work need not be lost; that is where they should be. Now put the foundations under them.

WALDEN

## AUGUST 12

I do not know but it is too much to read one newspaper a week. I have tried it recently, and for so long it seems to me that I have not dwelt in my native region. The sun, the clouds, the snow, the trees say not so much to me. You cannot serve two masters. It requires more than a day's devotion to know and to possess the wealth of a day. We may well be ashamed to tell what things we have read or heard in our day. I do not know why my news should be so trivial,—considering what one's dreams and expectations are, why the developments should be so paltry. The news we hear, for the most part, is not news to our genius. It is the stalest repetition. . . . We should wash ourselves clean of such news. Of what consequence, though our planet explode, if there is no character involved in the explosion? In health we have not the least curiosity about such events. We do not live for idle amusement. I would not run around the corner to see the world blow up.

LIFE WITHOUT PRINCIPLE

## AUGUST 13

If with closed ears and eyes I consult consciousness for a moment, immediately are all walls and barriers dissipated, earth rolls from under me, and I float, by the impetus derived from the earth and the system, a subjective, heavily laden thought, in the midst of an unknown and infinite sea, or else heave and swell like a vast ocean of thought, without rock or headland, where are all riddles solved, all straight lines making there their two ends to meet, eternity and space gambolling familiarly through my depths. I am from the beginning, knowing no end, no aim. No sun illumines me, for I dissolve all lesser lights in my own intenser and steadier light. I am a restful kernel in the magazine of the universe.

JOURNAL 1838

## AUGUST 14

When I go out of the house for a walk, uncertain as yet whither I will bend my steps, and submit myself to my instinct to decide for me, I find, strange and whimsical as it may seem, that I finally and inevitably settle southwest, toward some particular wood or meadow or deserted pasture or hill in that direction. My needle is slow to settle—varies a few degrees, and does not always point due south-west, it is true, and it has good authority for this variation, but it always settles between west and south-south-west. The future lies that way to me, and the earth seems more unexhausted and richer on that side. The outline which would bound my walks would be, not a circle, but a parabola, or rather like one of those cometary orbits which have been thought to be non-returning curves, in this case opening westward, in which my house occupies the place of the sun. I turn round and round irresolute sometimes for a quarter of an hour, until I decide for a thousandth time, that I will walk in the south-west or west. Eastward I go only by force; but westward I go free.

WALKING

## AUGUST 15

I find the actual to be far less real to me than the imagined. Why this singular prominence and importance is given to the former, I do not know. In proportion as that which possesses my thoughts is removed from the actual, it impresses me. I have never met with anything so truly visionary and accidental as some actual events. They have affected me less than my dreams. Whatever actually happens to a man is wonderfully trivial and insignificant,—even to death itself, I imagine. . . . This stream of events which we consent to call actual, and that other mightier stream which alone carries us with it,—what makes the difference? On the one our bodies float, and we have sympathy with it through them; on the other, our spirits. We are ever dying to one world and being born into another. . . . Our thoughts are the epochs of our life: all else is but as a journal of the winds that blew while we were here.

JOURNAL 1850

## AUGUST 16

Yet, for my part, I was never unusually squeamish; I could sometimes eat a fried rat with a good relish, if it were necessary. I am glad to have drunk water so long, for the same reason that I prefer the natural sky to an opium-eater's heaven. I would fain keep sober always; and there are infinite degrees of drunkenness. I believe that water is the only drink for a wise man; wine is not so noble a liquor; and think of dashing the hopes of a morning with a cup of warm coffee, or of an evening with a dish of tea! Ah, how low I fall when I am tempted by them! Even music may be intoxicating. Such apparently slight causes destroyed Greece and Rome, and will destroy England and America. Of all ebriosity, who does not prefer to be intoxicated by the air he breathes? I have found it to be the most serious objection to coarse labors long continued, that they compelled me to eat and drink coarsely also. But to tell the truth, I find myself at present somewhat less particular in these respects. I carry less religion to the table, ask no blessing; not because I am wiser than I was, but, I am obliged to confess, because, however much it is to be regretted, with years I have grown more coarse and indifferent.

WALDEN

## AUGUST 17

My heart leaps into my mouth at the sound of the wind in the woods. I, whose life was but yesterday so desultory and shallow, suddenly recover my spirits, my spirituality, through my hearing. Ah! if I could so live that there should be no desultory moment in all my life! that in the trivial season, when small fruits are ripe, my fruits might be ripe also! that I could match nature always with my moods! that in each season when some part of nature especially flourishes, then a corresponding part of me may not fail to flourish! Ah! I would walk, I would sit and sleep, with natural piety! What if I could pray aloud or to myself as I went along by the brooksides a cheerful prayer like the birds! For joy I could embrace the earth; I shall delight to be buried in it. . . . I thank you God. I do not deserve anything. I am unworthy of the least regard and yet I am made to rejoice. I am impure and worthless, and yet the world is gilded for my delight and holidays are prepared for me, and my path is strewn with flowers. But I cannot thank the Giver. I cannot even whisper my thanks to those human friends I have. It seems to me that I am more rewarded for my expectations than for anything I do or can do.

JOURNAL 1851

## AUGUST 18

What means this sense of lateness that so comes over one now,—as if the rest of the year were down-hill, and if we had not performed anything before, we should not now? The season of flowers or of promise may be said to be over, and now is the season of fruits; but where is our fruit? The night of the year is approaching. What have we done with our talent? All nature prompts and reproves us. How early in the year it begins to be late! The sound of the crickets, even in the spring, makes our hearts beat with its awful reproof, while it encourages with its seasonable warning. It matters not by how little we have fallen behind; it seems irretrievably late. The year is full of warnings of its shortness, as is life. The sound of so many insects and the sight of so many flowers affect us so,—the creek of the cricket and the sight of the prunella and autumnal dandelion. They say, "For the night cometh in which no man may work."

## AUGUST 19

Perhaps I am more than usually jealous with respect to my freedom. I feel that my connection with and obligation to society are still very slight and transient. Those slight labors which afford me a livelihood, and by which it is allowed that I am to some extent serviceable to my contemporaries, are as yet commonly a pleasure to me, and I am not often reminded that they are a necessity. So far I am successful. But I foresee that if my wants should be much increased, the labor required to supply them would become a drudgery. If I should sell both my forenoons and afternoons to society, as most appear to do, I am sure that, for me, there would be nothing left worth living for. I trust that I shall never thus sell my birthright for a mess of pottage. I wish to suggest that a man may be very industrious, and yet not spend his time well. There is no more fatal blunderer than he who consumes the greater part of his life getting his living. All great enterprises are self-supporting. . . . You must get your living by loving.

## AUGUST 20

Most men, even in this comparatively free country, through mere ignorance and mistake, are so occupied with the factitious cares and superfluously coarse labors of life that its finer fruits cannot be plucked by them. Their fingers, from excessive toil, are too clumsy and tremble too much for that. Actually, the laboring man has not leisure for a true integrity day by day; he cannot afford to sustain the manliest relations to men; his labor would be depreciated in the market. He has no time to be anything but a machine. How can he remember well his ignorance—which his growth requires—who has so often to use his knowledge? We should feed and clothe him gratuitously sometimes, and recruit him with our cordials, before we judge of him. The finest qualities of our nature, like the bloom on fruits, can be preserved only by the most delicate handling. Yet we do not treat ourselves nor one another thus tenderly.

WALDEN

## AUGUST 21

Why not live a hard and emphatic life, not to be avoided, full of adventures and work, learn much in it, travel much, though it be only I these woods? I sometimes walk across a field with unexpected expansion and long-missed content, as if there were a field worthy of me. The usual daily boundaries of life are dispersed, and I see in what field I stand. When on my way this afternoon, Shall I go down this long hill in the rain to fish in the pond? I ask myself. And I say to myself: Yes, roam far, grasp life and conquer it, learn much and live. Your fetters are knocked off; you are really free. Stay till late in the night;

be unwise and daring. . . . Do not repose every night as villagers do. The noble life is continuous and uninter-mitting. At least, live with a longer radius. . . . But come home from far, from ventures and perils, from enterprise and discovery and crusading, with faith and experience and character. Do not rest much. Dismiss prudence, fear, conformity. Remember only what is promised. Make the day light you, and the night hold a candle, though you be falling from heaven to earth "from morn to dewy eve a summer's day."

JOURNAL 1845

## AUGUST 22

Like many of my contemporaries, I had rarely for many years used animal food, or tea, or coffee, etc.; not so much because of any ill effects which I had traced to them, as because they were not agreeable to my imagi-nation. The repugnance to animal food is not the effect of experience, but is an instinct. It appeared more beau-tiful to live low and fare hard in many respects; and though I never did so, I went far enough to please my imagination. I believe that every man who has ever been earnest to preserve his higher or poetic faculties in the best condition has been particularly inclined to abstain from animal food, and from much food of any kind. . . . Whatever my own practice may be, I have no doubt that it is a part of the destiny of the human race, in its grad-ual improvement, to leave off eating animals, as surely as the savage tribes have left off eating each other when they came in contact with the more civilized.

WALDEN

## AUGUST 23

Live in each season as it passes; breathe the air, drink the drink, taste the fruit, and resign yourself to the influences of each. Let them be your only diet drink and botanical medicines. In August live on berries, not dried meats and pemmican, as if you were on shipboard making your way through a waste ocean, or in a northern desert. Be blown on by all the winds. Open all your pores and bathe in all the tides of Nature, in all her streams and oceans, at all seasons. Miasma and infection are from within, not without. . . . Grow green with the spring, yellow and ripe with autumn. Drink of each season's influence as a vial, a true panacea of all remedies mixed for your especial use. The vials of summer never made a man sick, but those which he stored in his cellar. Drink the wines, not of your bottling, but Nature's bottling; not kept in goat-skins or pig-skins, but the skins of a myriad fair berries. Let Nature do your bottling and your pickling and preserving. For all Nature is doing her best each moment to make us well. She exists for no other end. Do not resist her. With the least inclination to be well, we should not be sick. Men have discovered—or think they have discovered—the salutariness of a few wild things only, and not of all nature. Why, "nature" is but another name for health, and the seasons are but different states of health.

## AUGUST 24

With a little more deliberation in the choice of their pursuits, all men would perhaps become essentially students and observers, for certainly their nature and destiny are interesting to all alike. In accumulating property for ourselves or our posterity, in founding a family or a state, or acquiring fame even, we are mortal; but in dealing with truth we are immortal, and need fear no change nor accident. The oldest Egyptian or Hindoo philosopher raised a corner of the veil from the statue of the divinity; and still the trembling robe remains raised, and I gaze upon as fresh a glory as he did, since it was I in him that was then so bold, and it is he in me that now reviews the vision. No dust has settled on that robe; no time has elapsed since that divinity was revealed. That time which we really improve, or which is improvable, is neither past, present, nor future.

WALDEN

## AUGUST 25

Do a little more of that work which you have sometime confessed to be good—which you feel that society and your justest judge rightly demands of you. Do what you reprove yourself for not doing. Know that you are neither satisfied or dissatisfied with yourself without reason. Let me say to you and myself in one breath: Cultivate the tree which you have found to bear fruit in your soil. Regard not your past failures nor successes—all the past is equally a failure and a success. It is a success in as much as it offers you the present opportunity.... Do not trouble yourself to be religious; you will never get a thank you for it. If you can drive a nail and have any nails to drive, drive them. If you have any experiments you would like to try, try them; now's your chance. Do not entertain doubts, if they are not agreeable to you. ... Do not eat unless you are hungry; there's no need of it. Do not read the newspapers. Improve every opportunity to be melancholy. Be as melancholy as you can be, and note the result. Rejoice with fate. As for health, consider yourself well, and mind your business. Who knows but you are dead already? Do not stop to be scared yet; there are more terrible things to come, and ever to come. Men die of fright and live of confidence. ... Do not engage to find things as you think they are. Do what nobody can do for you. Omit to do everything else.

JOURNAL 1850


## AUGUST 26

I think that I cannot preserve my health and spirits unless I spend four hours a day at least —and it is commonly more than that—sauntering through the woods and over the hills and fields absolutely free from all worldly engagements. You may safely say a penny for your thoughts, or a thousand pounds. When sometimes I am reminded that the mechanics and shop-keepers stay in their shops not only all the forenoon, but all the afternoon too, sitting with crossed legs, so many of them—as if the legs were made to sit upon, and not to stand or walk upon—I think that they deserve some credit for not having all committed suicide long ago.

WALKING

## AUGUST 27

I have found repeatedly, of late years, that I cannot fish without falling a little in self-respect. I have tried it again and again. I have skill at it, and, like many of my fellows, a certain instinct for it, which revives from time to time, but always when I have done I feel that it would have been better if I had not fished. . . . There is unquestionably this instinct in me which belongs to the lower orders of creation; yet with every year I am less a fisherman, though without more humanity or even wisdom; at present I am no fisherman at all. But I see that if I were to live in a wilderness I should again be tempted to become a fisher and hunter in earnest. Beside, there is something essentially unclean about this diet and all flesh. . . . The practical objection to animal food in my case was its uncleaness; and besides, when I had caught and cleaned and cooked and eaten my fish, they seemed not to have fed me essentially.

WALDEN

## AUGUST 28

It is these comparatively cheap and private expeditions that substantiate our existence and batten our lives, as, where a vine touches the earth in its undulating course, it puts forth roots and thickens its stock. Our employment generally is tinkering, mending the old worn-out teapot of society. Our stock in trade is solder. Better for me, says my genius, to go cranberrying this afternoon . . . in Gowing's Swamp, to get but a pocketful and learn its peculiar flavor, aye, and the flavor of Gowing's Swamp and of *life* in New England, than to go consul to Liverpool and get I don't know how many thousand dollars for it, with no such flavor. Many of our days should be spent, not in vain expectations and lying on our oars, but in carrying out deliberately and faithfully the hundred little purposes which every man's genius must have suggested to him. Let not your life be wholly without an object, though it be only to ascertain the flavor of a cranberry, for it will not be only the quality of an insignificant berry that you will have tasted, but the flavor of your life to that extent, and it will be such a sauce as no wealth can buy.

JOURNAL 1856


## AUGUST 29

As with our colleges, so with a hundred "modern improvements"; there is an illusion about them; there is not always a positive advance. The devil goes on exacting compound interest to the last for his early share and numerous succeeding investments in them. Our inventions are wont to be pretty toys, which distract our attention from serious things. They are but improved means to an unimproved end, an end which it was already but too easy to arrive at; as railroads lead to Boston or New York. We are in great haste to construct a magnetic telegraph from Maine to Texas; but Maine and Texas, it may be, have nothing important to communicate. Either is in such a predicament as the man who was earnest to be introduced to a distinguished deaf woman, but when he was presented, and one end of her ear trumpet was put into his hand, had nothing to say. As if the main object were to talk fast and not to talk sensibly. We are eager to tunnel under the Atlantic and bring the Old World some weeks nearer to the New; but perchance the first news that will leak through into the broad, flapping American ear will be that the Princess Adelaide has the whooping cough. After all, the man whose horse trots a mile in a minute does not carry the most important messages.

WALDEN

## AUGUST 30

Both a conscious and an unconscious life are good. Neither is good exclusively, for both have the same source. The wisely conscious life springs out of an unconscious suggestion. I have found my account in having prepared beforehand a list of questions which I would get answered, not trusting to my interest at the moment, and can then travel with the most profit. Indeed, it is by obeying the suggestion of a higher light within you that you escape from yourself and, in the transit, as it were, see with the unworn sides of your eye, travel totally new paths. What is that pretended life that does not take up a claim, that does not occupy ground, that cannot build a causeway to its objects, that sits on a bank looking over a bog, singing its desires?

JOURNAL 1856

## AUGUST 31

The stillness was intense and almost conscious, as if it were a natural Sabbath, and we fancied that the morning was the evening of a celestial day. The air was so elastic and crystalline that it had the same effect on the landscape that a glass has on a picture, to give it an ideal remoteness and perfection. The landscape was clothed in a mild and quiet light, in which the woods and fences checkered and partitioned it with new regularity, and rough and uneven fields stretched away with lawn-like smoothness to the horizon, and the clouds, finely distinct and picturesque, seemed a fit drapery to hang over fairy-land. The world seemed decked for some holiday or prouder pageantry, with silken streamers flying, and the course of our lives to wind on before us like a green lane into a country maze, at the season when fruit-trees are in blossom.

**A WEEK ON THE CONCORD & MERRIMACK RIVERS**

SEPTEMBER

## SEPTEMBER 1

The savage lives simply through ignorance and idleness or laziness, but the philosopher lives simply through wisdom. In the case of the savage, the accompaniment of simplicity is idleness with its attendant vices, but in the case of the philosopher, it is the highest employment and development. The fact for the savage, and for the mass of mankind, is that it is better to plant, weave, and build than do nothing or worse; but the fact for the philosopher, or a nation loving wisdom, is that it is most important to cultivate the highest faculties and spend as little time as possible in planting, weaving, building, etc. It depends upon the height of your standard. . . . There are two kinds of simplicity,—one that is akin to foolishness, the other to wisdom. The philosopher's style of living is only outwardly simple, but inwardly complex. The savage's style is both outwardly and inwardly simple. . . . A man who has equally limited views with respect to the end of living will not be helped by the most complex and refined style of living. It is not the tub that makes Diogenes, the Jove-born, but Diogenes the tub.

JOURNAL 1853

## SEPTEMBER 2

As we sat on the bank eating our supper, the clear light of the western sky fell on the eastern trees, and was reflected in the water, and we enjoyed so serene an evening as left nothing to describe. For the most part we think that there are few degrees of sublimity, and that the highest is but little higher than that which we now behold; but we are always deceived. Sublimer visions appear, and the former pale and fade away. We are grateful when we are reminded by interior evidence of the permanence of universal laws, for our faith is but faintly remembered, indeed, is not a remembered assurance, but a use and enjoyment of knowledge. It is when we do not have to believe, but come into actual contact with Truth, and are related to her in the most direct and intimate way. Waves of serener life pass over us from time to time, like flakes of sunlight over the fields in cloudy weather.

A WEEK ON THE CONCORD & MERRIMACK RIVERS

## SEPTEMBER 3

There were times when I could not afford to sacrifice the bloom of the present moment to any work, whether of the head or hands. I love a broad margin to my life. Sometimes, in a summer morning, having taken my accustomed bath, I sat in my sunny doorway from sunrise till noon, rapt in a revery, amidst the pines and hickories and sumachs, in undisturbed solitude and stillness, while the birds sang around or flitted noiseless through the house, until by the sun falling in at my west window, or the noise of some traveller's wagon on the distant highway, I was reminded of the lapse of time. I grew in those seasons like corn in the night, and they were far better than any work of the hands would have been. They were not time subtracted from my life, but so much over and above my usual allowance. I realized what the Orientals mean by contemplation and the forsaking of works.

WALDEN

## SEPTEMBER 4

I wish my countrymen to consider, that whatever the human law may be, neither an individual nor a nation can ever commit the least act of injustice against the obscurest individual without having to pay the penalty for it. A government which deliberately enacts injustice, and persists in it, will at length ever become the laughing-stock of the world.... The law will never make men free; it is men who have got to make the law free. They are the lovers of law and order who observe the law when the government breaks it.

SLAVERY IN MASSACHUSETTS

## SEPTEMBER 5

How to live. How to get the most life. As if you were to teach the young hunter how to entrap his game. How to extract its honey from the flower of the world. That is my every-day business. I am as busy as a bee about it. I ramble over all fields on that errand, and am never so happy as when I feel myself heavy with honey and wax. I am like a bee searching the livelong day for the sweets of nature. Do I not impregnate and intermix the flowers, produce rare and finer varieties by transferring my eyes from one to another? With what honeyed thought any experience yields me I take a bee line to my cell. It is with flowers I would deal. Where is the flower, there is the honey. . . . So by the dawning or radiance of beauty are we advertised where is the honey and the fruit of thought, of discourse, and of action. We are first attracted by the beauty of the flower, before we discover the honey which is a foretaste of the future fruit.

JOURNAL 1851

## SEPTEMBER 6

John Farmer sat at his door one September evening, after a hard day's work, his mind still running on his labor more or less. Having bathed, he sat down to recreate his intellectual man. It was a rather cool evening, and some of his neighbors were apprehending a frost. He had not attended to the train of his thoughts long when he heard some one playing on a flute, and that sound harmonized with his mood. Still he thought of his work; but the burden of his thought was, that though this kept running in his head, and he found himself planning and contriving it against his will, yet it concerned him very little. It was no more than the scurf of his skin, which was constantly shuffled off. But the notes of the flute came home to his ears out of a different sphere from that he worked in, and suggested work for certain faculties which slumbered in him. They gently did away with the street, and the village, and the state in which he lived. A voice said to him,—Why do you stay here and live this mean moiling life, when a glorious existence is possible for you? Those same stars twinkle over other fields than these.—But how to come out of this condition and actually migrate thither? All that he could think of was to practise some new austerity, to let his mind descend into his body and redeem it, and treat himself with ever increasing respect.

## SEPTEMBER 7

Our ecstatic states, which appear to yield so little fruit, have this value at least: though in the seasons when our genius reigns we may be powerless for expression, yet, in calmer seasons, when our talent is active, the memory of those rarer moods comes to color our picture and is the permanent paint-pot, as it were, into which we dip our brush. Thus no life of experience goes unreported at last; but if it be not solid gold it is gold-leaf which gilds the furniture of the mind. It is an experience of infinite beauty on which we unfailingly draw, which enables us to exaggerate ever truly. Our moments of inspiration are not lost though we have no particular poem to show for them; for those experiences have left an indelible impression, and we are ever and anon reminded of them. Their truth subsides, and in cooler moments we can use them as paint to gild and adorn our prose. . . . We are receiving our portion of the infinite. The art of life! Was there ever anything memorable written upon it? By what disciplines to secure the most life, with what care to watch our thoughts. To observe what transpires, not in the street, but in the mind and heart of me! I do not remember any page which will tell me how to spend his afternoon. I do not so much wish to know how to economize time as how to spend it, by what means to grow rich, that the day may not have been in vain.

## SEPTEMBER 8

I am affected by the thought that the earth nurses these eggs. They are planted in the earth, and the earth takes care of them; she is genial to them and does not kill them. It suggests a certain vitality and intelligence in the earth, which I had not realized. This mother is not merely inanimate and inorganic. Though the immediate mother turtle abandons her offspring, the earth and sun are kind to them. The old turtle on which the earth rests takes care of them while the other waddles off. Earth was not made poisonous and deadly to them. The earth has some virtue in it; when seeds are put into it, they germinate; when turtles' eggs, they hatch in due time. Though the mother turtle remained and brooded them, it would still nevertheless be the universal world turtle which, through her, cared for them as now. Thus the earth is the mother of all creatures.

## SEPTEMBER 9

Your scheme must be the framework of the universe; all other schemes will soon be ruins. The perfect God in his revelations of himself has never got to the length of one such proposition as you, his prophets, state. Have you learned the alphabet of heaven and can count three? Do you know the number of God's family? Can you put mysteries into words? Do you presume to fable of the ineffable? Pray, what geographer are you, that speak of heaven's topography? Whose friend are you that speak of God's personality? Do you, Miles Howard, think that he has made you his confidant? Tell me of the height of the mountains of the moon, or of the diameter of space, and I may believe you, but of the secret history of the Almighty, and I shall pronounce thee mad. Yet we have a sort of family history of our God,—so have the Tahitians of theirs,—and some old poet's grand imagination is imposed on us as adamantine everlasting truth, and God's own word!

A WEEK ON THE CONCORD & MERRIMACK RIVERS

## SEPTEMBER 10

But I say that I have no scheme about it,—no designs on men at all; and, if I had, my mode would be to tempt them with the fruit, and not with the manure. To what end do I lead a simple life at all, pray? That I may teach others to simplify their lives?—and so all our lives be *simplified* merely, like an algebraic formula? Or not, rather, that I may make use of the ground I have cleared, to live more worthily and profitably? I would fain lay the most stress forever on that which is the most important, —imports the most to me,—though it were only . . . a vibration in the air. As a preacher, I should be prompted to tell men, not so much how to get their wheat-bread cheaper, as of the bread of life compared with which *that* is bran. Let a man only taste these loaves, and he becomes a skillful economist at once.

LETTERS 1855


## SEPTEMBER 11

I wish to speak a word for Nature, for absolute freedom and wildness, as contrasted with a freedom and culture merely civil,—to regard man as an inhabitant, or part and parcel of Nature, rather than a member of society. I wish to make an extreme statement, if so I may make an emphatic one, for there are enough champions of civilization: the minister and the school-committee and every one of you will take care of that.

WALKING


## SEPTEMBER 12

At the entrance to the Deep Cut, I heard the telegraph-wire vibrating like an aeolian harp. It reminded me suddenly,—reservedly, with a beautiful paucity of communication, even silently, such was its effect on my thoughts,—it reminded me, I say, with a certain pathetic moderation, of what finer and deeper stirrings I was susceptible, which grandly set all argument and dispute aside, a triumphant though transient exhibition of the truth. It told me by the faintest imaginable strain, it told me by the finest strain that a human ear can hear, yet conclusively and past all refutation, that there were higher, infinitely higher, planes of life which it behooved me never to forget. As I was entering the Deep Cut, the wind, which was conveying a message to me from heaven, dropped it on the wire of the telegraph which it vibrated as it passed. I instantly sat down on a stone at the foot of the telegraph-pole, and attended to the communication. It merely said: "Bear in mind, Child, and never for an instant forget, that there are higher planes, infinitely higher planes, of life than this thou art now travelling on. Know that the goal is distant, and is upward, and is worthy all your life's efforts to attain to." And then it ceased, and though I sat some minutes longer I heard nothing more.

JOURNAL 1851

## SEPTEMBER 13

I must walk more with free senses. It is as bad to *study* stars and clouds as flowers and stones. I must let my senses wander as my thoughts, my eyes see without looking. Carlyle said that how to observe was to look, but I say that it is rather to see, and the more you look the less you will observe. I have the habit of attention to such an excess that my senses get no rest, but suffer from a constant strain. Be not preoccupied with looking. Go not to the object; let it come to you. When I have found myself ever looking down and confining my gaze to the flowers, I have thought it might be well to get into the habit of observing the clouds as a corrective; but no! that study would be just as bad. What I need is not to look at all, but a true sauntering of the eye.

JOURNAL 1852

## SEPTEMBER 14

In our most trivial walks, we are constantly, though unconsciously, steering like pilots by certain well-known beacons and headlands, and if we go beyond our usual course we still carry in our minds the bearing of some neighboring cape; and not till we are completely lost, or turned round—for a man needs only to be turned round once with his eyes shut in this world to be lost—do we appreciate the vastness and strangeness of nature. Every man has to learn the points of compass again as often as he awakes, whether from sleep or any abstraction. Not till we are lost, in other words, not till we have lost the world, do we begin to find ourselves, and realize where we are and the extent of our relations.

WALDEN

## SEPTEMBER 15

What a difference, whether, in all your walks, you meet only strangers, or in one house is one who knows you, and whom you know. To have a brother or a sister! To have a gold mine on your farm! To find diamonds in the gravel heaps before your door! How rare these things are! To share the day with you,—to people the earth. Whether to have a god or a goddess for companion in your walks, or to walk alone with hinds and villains and carles. Would not a friend enhance the beauty of the landscape as much as a deer or hare? Everything would acknowledge and serve such a relation; the corn in the field, and the cranberries in the meadow. The flowers would bloom, and the birds sing, with a new impulse. There would be more fair days in the year.

LETTERS 1852

## SEPTEMBER 16

The art of spending a day. If it is possible that we may be addressed, it behooves us to be attentive. If by watching all day and all night I may detect some trace of the Ineffable, then will it not be worth the while to watch? Watch and pray without ceasing, but not necessarily in sadness. Be of good cheer. . . . I am convinced that men are not well employed, that this is not the way to spend a day. If by patience, if by watching, I can secure one new ray of light, can feel myself elevated for an instant upon Pisgah, the world which was dead prose to me become living and divine, shall I not watch ever? shall I not be a watchman henceforth? If by watching a whole year on the city's walls I may obtain a communication from heaven, shall I not do well to shut up my shop and turn a watchman?

Can a youth, a man, do more wisely than to go where his life is to be found? As if I had suffered that to be rumor which may be verified. We are surrounded by a rich and fertile mystery. May we not probe it, pry into it, employ ourselves about it, a little? To devote your life to the study of the divinity in nature or to the eating of oysters, would they not be attended with very different results?

JOURNAL 1851

## SEPTEMBER 17

I was once reproved by a minister . . . because I was bending my steps to a mountain-top on the Sabbath, instead of a church, when I would have gone farther than he to hear a true word spoken on that or any day. He declared that I was "breaking the Lord's fourth commandment," and proceeded to enumerate, in a sepulchral tone, the disasters which had befallen him whenever he had done any ordinary work on the Sabbath. He really thought that a god was on the watch to trip up those men who followed any secular work on this day, and did not see that it was the evil conscience of the workers that did it. The country is full of this superstition, so that when one enters a village, the church, not only really but from association, is the ugliest looking building in it, because it is the one in which human nature stoops the lowest and is most disgraced. Certainly, such temples as these shall erelong cease to deform the landscape.

**A WEEK ON THE CONCORD & MERRIMACK RIVERS**

## SEPTEMBER 18

There is commonly sufficient space about us. Our horizon is never quite at our elbows. The thick wood is not just at our door, nor the pond, but somewhat is always clearing, familiar and worn by us, appropriated and fenced in some way, and reclaimed from Nature. For what reason have I this vast range and circuit, some square miles of unfrequented forest, for my privacy, abandoned to me by men? My nearest neighbor is a mile distant, and no house is visible from any place but the hill-tops within half a mile of my own. I have my horizon bounded by woods all to myself; a distant view of the railroad where it touches the pond on the one hand, and of the fence which skirts the woodland road on the other. But for the most part it is as solitary where I live as on the prairies. It is as much Asia or Africa as New England. I have, as it were, my own sun and moon and stars, and a little world all to myself.

WALDEN

## SEPTEMBER 19

Thinking this afternoon of the prospect of my writing lectures and going abroad to read them the next winter, I realized how incomparably great the advantages of obscurity and poverty which I have enjoyed so long (and may still perhaps enjoy). I thought with what more than princely, with what poetical leisure I had spent my years hitherto, without care or engagement, fancy-free. I have given myself up to nature; I have lived so many springs and summers and autumns and winters as if I had nothing else to do but *live* them and imbibe whatever nutriment they had for me; I have spent a couple of years, for instance, with the flowers chiefly, having none other so binding engagement as to observe when they opened; I could have afforded to spend a whole fall observing the changing tints of the foliage. Ah, how I have thriven on solitude and poverty! I cannot overstate this advantage. I do not see how I could have enjoyed it, if the public had been expecting as much of me as there is danger now that they will. If I go abroad lecturing, how shall I ever recover the lost winter? It has been my vacation, my season of growth and expansion, a prolonged youth.

JOURNAL 1854

## SEPTEMBER 20

This was that Earth of which we have heard, made out of Chaos and Old Night. Here was no man's garden, but the unhandselled globe. It was not lawn, nor pasture, nor mead, nor woodland, nor lea, nor arable, nor wasteland. It was the fresh and natural surface of the planet Earth, as it was made for-ever and ever,—to be the dwelling of man, we say,—so Nature made it, and man may use it if he can. Man was not to be associated with it. It was Matter, vast, terrific,—not his Mother Earth that we have heard of, not for him to tread on, or be buried in,—no, it were being too familiar even to let his bones lie there,—the home, this, of Necessity and Fate.

There was there felt the presence of a force not bound to be kind to man. It was a place for heathenism and super-stitious rites,—to be inhabited by men nearer kin to the rocks and to wild animals than we. We walked over it with a certain awe, stopping, from time to time, to pick the blueberries which grew there, and had a smart and spicy taste. Perchance where *our* wild pines stand, and leaves lie on their forest floor, in Concord, there were once reapers, and husbandmen planted grain; but here not even the surface had been scarred by man, but it was a specimen of what God saw fit to make this world. . . . I stand in awe of my body, this matter to which I am bound has become so strange to me. I fear not spirits, ghosts, of which I am one,—*that* my body might,—but I fear bodies, I tremble to meet them. What is this Titan that has possession of me? Talk of mysteries! Think of our life in nature,—daily to be shown matter, to come in contact with it,—rocks, trees, wind on our cheeks! the *solid* earth! the *actual* world! the *common sense*! *Contact! Contact! Who* are we? *where* are we?

THE MAINE WOODS

## SEPTEMBER 21

The sun sets on some retired meadow, where no house is visible, with all the glory and splendor that it lavishes on cities, and perchance, as it has never set before,—where there is but a solitary marsh hawk to have his wings gilded by it, or only a musquash looks out from his cabin, and there is some little black-veined brook in the midst of the marsh, just beginning to meander, winding slowly round a decaying stump. We walked in so pure and bright a light, gilding the withered grass and leaves, so softly and serenely bright I thought I had never bathed in such a golden flood, without a ripple or a murmur to it. The west side of every wood and rising ground gleamed like the boundary of elysium, and the sun on our backs seemed like a gentle herdsman, driving us home at evening. So we saunter toward the Holy Land; till one day the sun shall shine more brightly than ever he has done, shall perchance shine into our minds and hearts, and light up our whole lives with a great awakening light, so warm and serene and golden as on a bank-side in Autumn.

WALKING

## SEPTEMBER 22

What if we were to walk by sunlight with equal abstraction and aloofness, yet with equally impartial observation and criticism. As if it shone not for you, nor you for it, but you had come forth into it for the nonce to admire it. By moonlight we are not of the earth earthy, but we are of the earth spiritual. So might we walk by sunlight, seeing the sun but as a moon, a comparatively faint and reflected light, and the day as a brooding night, in which we glimpse some stars still. . . . By moonlight all is simple. We are enabled to erect ourselves, our minds, on account of the fewness of objects. We are no longer distracted. It is simple as bread and water. It is simple as the rudiments of an art,—a lesson to be taken before sunlight, perchance, to prepare us for that.

## SEPTEMBER 23

As we have said, Nature is a greater and more perfect art, the art of God; though, referred to herself, she is genius, and there is a similarity between her operations and man's art even in the details and trifles. When the overhanging pine drops into the water, by the sun and water, and the wind rubbing it against the shore, its boughs are worn into fantastic shapes, and white and smooth, as if turned in a lathe. Man's art has wisely imitated those forms into which all matter is most inclined to run, as foliage and fruit. A hammock swung in a grove assumes the exact form of a canoe, broader or narrower, and higher or lower at the ends, as more or fewer persons are in it, and it rolls in the air with the motion of the body, like a canoe in the water. Our art leaves its shavings and its dust about; her art exhibits itself even in the shavings and the dust which we make. She has perfected herself by an eternity of practice. The world is well kept; no rubbish accumulates; the morning air is clear even at this day, and no dust has settled on the grass.

## SEPTEMBER 24

Men think that it is essential that the *Nation* have commerce, and export ice, and talk through a telegraph, and ride thirty miles an hour, without a doubt, whether *they* do or not; but whether we should live like baboons or like men, is a little uncertain. If we do not get out sleepers, and forge rails, and devote days and nights to the work, but go to tinkering upon our *lives* to improve *them*, who will build railroads? And if railroads are not built, how shall we get to heaven in season? But if we stay at home and mind our business, who will want railroads? We do not ride on the railroad; it rides upon us. Did you ever think what those sleepers are that underlie the railroad? Each one is a man, an Irishman, or a Yankee man. The rails are laid on them, and they are covered with sand, and the cars run smoothly over them. They are sound sleepers, I assure you.

WALDEN

## SEPTEMBER 25

What the essential difference between man and woman is, that they should be thus attracted to one another, no one has satisfactorily answered. Perhaps we must acknowledge the justness of the distinction which assigns to man the sphere of wisdom, and to woman that of love, though neither belongs exclusively to either. Man is continually saying to woman, Why will you not be more wise? Woman is continually saying to man, Why will you not be more loving? It is not in their wills to be wise or to be loving; but, unless each is both wise and loving, there can be neither wisdom nor love.

LETTERS 1852

## SEPTEMBER 26

There is a certain fertile sadness which I would not avoid, but rather earnestly seek. It is positively joyful to me. It saves my life from being trivial. My life flows with a deeper current, no longer as a shallow and brawling stream, parched and shrunken by the summer heats. . . . The stillness seems more deep and significant. Each sound seems to come from out a greater thoughtfulness in nature, as if nature had acquired some character and mind. The cricket, the gurgling stream, the rushing wind amid the trees, all speak to me soberly yet encouragingly of the steady onward progress of the universe.

JOURNAL 1851

## SEPTEMBER 27

This world has many rings, like Saturn, and we live now on the outmost of them all. None can say deliberately that he inhabits the same sphere, or is contemporary with, the flower which his hands have plucked, and though his feet may seem to crush it, inconceivable spaces and ages separate them, and perchance there is no danger that he will hurt it. What do the botanists know? Our lives should go between the lichen and the bark. The eye may see for the hand, but not for the mind. We are still being born, and have as yet but a dim vision of sea and land, sun, moon, and stars, and shall not see clearly till after nine days at least. That is a pathetic inquiry among travellers and geographers after the site of ancient Troy. It is not where they think it is. When a thing is decayed and gone, how indistinct must be the place it occupied.

A WEEK ON THE CONCORD & MERRIMACK RIVERS

## SEPTEMBER 28

Yet we should oftener look over the tafferel of our craft, like curious passengers, and not make the voyage like stupid sailors picking oakum. The other side of the globe is but the home of our correspondent. Our voyaging is only great-circle sailing, and the doctors prescribe for diseases of the skin merely. One hastens to southern Africa to chase the giraffe; but surely that is not the game he would be after. How long, pray, would a man hunt giraffes if he could? Snipes and woodcocks also may afford rare sport; but I trust it would be nobler game to shoot one's self.

"Direct your eye right inward, and you'll find
 A thousand regions in your mind
 Yet undiscovered. Travel them, and be
 Expert in home-cosmography."

WALDEN

## SEPTEMBER 29

Let the despairing race of men know that there is in Nature no sign of decay, but universal and uninterrupted vigor. All waste and ruin has a speedy period. Who ever detected a wrinkle on her brow, or a weather seam, or a grey hair on her crown, or a rent in her garment. No one sees nature, who sees her not as young and fresh, without history. We may have such intercourse today as we imagine to constitute the employment of gods. We live here to have intercourse with rivers, forests, mountains, beasts and men. How few do we see conversing with these things. We think the ancients were foolish who worshiped the sun. I would worship it forever if I had the grace to do so. Observe how a New England farmer moves in the midst of nature—his potato and grain fields—and consider how poets have dreamed that the more religious shepherd lived, and ask which is the wiser, which made the highest use of nature. As if the Earth were made to yield pumpkins mainly. Did you never observe that the seasons were ripening another kind of fruit?

JOURNAL 1843

 ## SEPTEMBER 30

I delight to come to my bearings,—not walk in procession with pomp and parade, in a conspicuous place but to walk even with the Builder of the universe, if I may,— not to live in this restless, nervous, bustling, trivial

Nineteenth Century, but stand or sit thoughtfully while it goes by. What are men celebrating? They are all on a committee of arrangements, and hourly expect a speech from somebody. God is only the president of the day, and Webster is his orator. I love to weigh, to settle, to gravitate toward that which most strongly and rightfully attracts me;—not hang by the beam of the scale and try to weigh less,—not suppose a case, but take the case that is; to travel the only path I can, and that on which no power can resist me. It affords me no satisfaction to commence to spring an arch before I have got a solid foundation. Let us not play at kittly-benders.

WALDEN

OCTOBER

# OCTOBER 1

Both place and time were changed, and I dwelt nearer to those parts of the universe and to those eras in history which had most attracted me. Where I lived was as far off as many a region viewed nightly by astronomers. We are wont to imagine rare and delectable places in some remote and more celestial corner of the system, behind the constellation of Cassiopeia's Chair, far from noise and disturbance. I discovered that my house actually had its site in such a withdrawn, but forever new and unprofaned, part of the universe. If it were worth the while to settle in those parts near to the Pleiades or the Hyades, to Aldebaran or Altair, then I was really there, or at an equal remoteness from the life which I had left behind, dwindled and twinkling with as fine a ray to my nearest neighbor, and to be seen only in moonless nights by him.

WALDEN

# OCTOBER 2

We have felt that we almost alone hereabouts practised this noble art; though, to tell the truth, at least, if their own assertions are to be received, most of my townsmen would fain walk sometimes, as I do, but they cannot. No wealth can buy the requisite leisure, freedom, and independence, which are the capital in this profession. It comes only by the grace of God. It requires a direct dispensation from heaven to become a walker. You must be born into the family of the Walkers. *Ambulator nascitur, non fit.* Some of my townsmen, it is true, can remember, and have described to me some walks which they took ten years ago, in which they were so blessed as to lose themselves for half an hour in the woods, but I know very well that they have confined themselves to the highway ever since, whatever pretensions they may make to belong to this select class. No doubt, they were elevated for a moment as by the reminiscence of a previous state of existence, when even they were foresters and outlaws.

WALKING

## OCTOBER 3

Why does any distant prospect ever charm us? Because we instantly and inevitably imagine a life to be lived there such as is not lived elsewhere, or where we are. We presume that success is the rule. We forever carry a perfect sampler in our minds. Why are distant valleys, why lakes, why mountains in the horizon, ever fair to us? Because we realize for a moment that they may be the home of man, and that man's life may be in harmony with them. Shall I say that we thus forever delude ourselves? We do not suspect that *that* farmer goes to the depot with his milk. *There* the milk is not watered. We are constrained to imagine a life in harmony with the scenery and the hour. The sky and clouds, and the earth itself, with their beauty forever preach to us, saying, Such an abode we offer you, to such and such a life we encourage you. *There* is not haggard poverty and harassing debt. There is not intemperance, moroseness, meanness, or vulgarity. Men go about sketching, painting land-scapes, or writing verses which celebrate man's opportu-nities. . . . There is no beauty in the sky, but in the eye that sees it. Health, high spirits, serenity, these are the great landscape-painters. Turners, Claudes, Rembrandts are nothing to them.

## OCTOBER 4

It is only when we forget all our learning that we begin to know. I do not get nearer by a hair's breadth to any natural object so long as I presume that I have an intro-duction to it from some learned man. To conceive of it with a total apprehension I must for the thousandth time approach it as something totally strange. If you would make acquaintance with the ferns you must for-get your botany. You must get rid of what is commonly called *knowledge* of them. Not a single scientific term or distinction is the least to the purpose, for you would fain perceive something, and you must approach the object totally unprejudiced. You must be aware that *no thing* is what you have taken it to be. In what book is this world and its beauty described? Who has plotted the steps toward the discovery of beauty? You have got to be in a different state from common. Your greatest success will be simply to perceive that such things are, and you will have no communication to make to the Royal Society.

## OCTOBER 5

In such a day, in September or October, Walden is a perfect forest mirror, set round with stones as precious to my eye as if fewer or rarer. Nothing so fair, so pure, and at the same time so large, as a lake, perchance, lies on the surface of the earth. Sky water. It needs no fence. Nations come and go without defiling it. It is a mirror which no stone can crack, whose quicksilver will never wear off, whose gilding Nature continually repairs; no storms, no dust, can dim its surface ever fresh;—a mirror in which all impurity presented to it sinks, swept and dusted by the sun's hazy brush—this the light dust-cloth—which retains no breath that is breathed on it, but sends its own to float as clouds high above its surface, and be reflected in its bosom still.

WALDEN

## OCTOBER 6

Every man, if he is wise, will stand on such bottom as will sustain him, and if one gravitates downward more strongly than another, he will not venture on those meads where the latter walks securely, but rather leave the cranberries which grow there unraked by himself. Perchance, some spring a higher freshet will float them within his reach, though they may be watery and frost-bitten by that time. Such shrivelled berries I have seen in many a poor man's garret, ay, in many a church-bin and state-coffer, and with a little water and heat they swell again to their original size and fairness, and added sugar enough, stead mankind for sauce to this world's dish. What is called common sense is excellent in its department, and as invaluable as the virtue of conformity in the army and navy,—for there must be subordination,— but uncommon sense, that sense which is common only to the wisest, is as much more excellent as it is more rare.

A WEEK ON THE CONCORD & MERRIMACK RIVERS

## OCTOBER 7

There will never be a really free and enlightened State until the State comes to recognize the individual as a higher and independent power, from which all its own power and authority are derived, and treats him accordingly. I please myself with imagining a State at last which can afford to be just to all men, and to treat the individual with respect as a neighbor; which even would not think it inconsistent with its own repose if a few were to live aloof from it, not meddling with it, nor embraced by it, who fulfilled all the duties of neighbors and fellowmen. A State which bore this kind of fruit, and suffered it to drop off as fast as it ripened, would prepare the way for a still more perfect and glorious State, which also I have imagined, but not yet anywhere seen.

RESISTANCE TO CIVIL GOVERNMENT

## OCTOBER 8

There must be all degrees of life from a stone, if we can find any starting point, to God. There are very few fibres in the stone—very little organism. Sometimes we are conscious of the simple but slow and insensate life which it lives. We are mere pudding stone or scoriae in the world. But suddenly we may be informed with new life, and pass through all the scales of being up to the most complex and nearest to God, furnished with countless nerves and imbibing more and more of vital air or inspiration. How suddenly and silently do all the eras which we call history awaken and glimmer in us. All the dynasties that have past away are still passing in our memory. There is room for Alexander to march and for Hannibal to conquer. The grand three act drama of past, present and future, where does its scene lie but within the compass of this same private life which beats within its ribbed wall? We may say that our knowledge is finite— for we have never discovered its limits—and what we know of infinity is part of our knowledge still. History is the record of my experience. I can read only my own story, never a syllable of another's.

JOURNAL 1843

## OCTOBER 9

Time is but the stream I go a-fishing in. I drink at it; but while I drink I see the sandy bottom and detect how shallow it is. Its thin current slides away, but eternity remains. I would drink deeper; fish in the sky, whose bottom is pebbly with stars. I cannot count one. I know not the first letter of the alphabet. I have always been regretting that I was not as wise as the day I was born. The intellect is a cleaver; it discerns and rifts its way into the secret of things. I do not wish to be any more busy with my hands than is necessary. My head is hands and feet. I feel all my best faculties concentrated in it. My instinct tells me that my head is an organ for burrowing, as some creatures use their snout and fore-paws, and with it I would mine and burrow my way through these hills. I think that the richest vein is somewhere here-abouts; so by the divining rod and thin rising vapors I judge; and here I will begin to mine.

WALDEN

## OCTOBER 10

Just so hollow and ineffectual, for the most part, is our ordinary conversation. Surface meets surface. When our life ceases to be inward and private, conversation degenerates into mere gossip. We rarely meet a man who can tell us any news which he has not read in a newspaper, or been told by his neighbor; and, for the most part, the only difference between us and our fellow is, that he has seen the newspaper, or been out to tea, and we have not. In proportion as our inward life fails, we go more constantly and desperately to the post-office. You may depend on it, that the poor fellow who walks away with the greatest number of letters, proud of his extensive correspondence, has not heard from himself this long while.

LIFE WITHOUT PRINCIPLE

## OCTOBER 11

Men esteem truth remote, in the outskirts of the system, behind the farthest star, before Adam and after the last man. In eternity there is indeed something true and sublime. But all these times and places and occasions are now and here. God himself culminates in the present moment, and will never be more divine in the lapse of all the ages. And we are enabled to apprehend at all what is sublime and noble only by the perpetual instilling and drenching of the reality that surrounds us. The universe constantly and obediently answers to our conceptions; whether we travel fast or slow, the track is laid for us. Let us spend our lives in conceiving then. The poet or the artist never yet had so fair and noble a design but some of his posterity at least could accomplish it.

WALDEN

## OCTOBER 12

In vain I see the morning rise,
      In vain observe the western blaze,
Who idly look to other skies,
      Expecting life by other ways.

Amidst such boundless wealth without,
      I only still am poor within,
The birds have sung their summer out,
      But still my spring does not begin.

Shall I then wait the autumn wind,
　　Compelled to seek a milder day,
And leave no curious nest behind,
　　No woods still echoing to my lay?

A WEEK ON THE CONCORD & MERRIMACK RIVERS

## OCTOBER 13

I had this advantage, at least, in my mode of life, over those who were obliged to look abroad for amusement, to society and the theatre, that my life itself was become my amusement and never ceased to be novel. It was a drama of many scenes and without an end. If we were always, indeed, getting our living, and regulating our lives according to the last and best mode we had learned, we should never be troubled with ennui. Follow your genius closely enough, and it will not fail to show you a fresh prospect every hour. Housework was a pleasant pastime. When my floor was dirty, I rose early, and, setting all my furniture out of doors on the grass, bed and bedstead making but one budget, dashed water on the floor, and sprinkled white sand from the pond on it, and then with a broom scrubbed it clean and white; and by the time the villagers had broken their fast the morning sun had dried my house sufficiently to allow me to move in again, and my meditations were almost uninterrupted.

WALDEN

## OCTOBER 14

Life consists with Wildness. The most alive is the wildest. Not yet subdued to man, its presence refreshes him. One who pressed forward incessantly and never rested from his labors, who grew fast and made infinite demands on life, would always find himself in a new country or wilderness, and surrounded by the raw material of life. He would be climbing over the prostrate stems of primitive forest-trees. Hope and the future for me are not in lawns and cultivated fields, not in towns and cities, but in the impervious and quaking swamps. When, formerly, I have analyzed my partiality for some farm which I had contemplated purchasing, I have frequently found that I was attracted solely by a few square rods of impermeable and unfathomable bog,—a natural sink in one corner of it. That was the jewel that dazzled me. I derive more of my substance from the swamps which surround my native town than from the cultivated gardens in the village.

WALKING

## OCTOBER 15

Each town should have a park, or rather a primitive forest, of five hundred or a thousand acres, where a stick should never be cut for fuel, a common possession forever, for instruction and recreation. We hear of cow-commons and ministerial lots, but we want *men*-commons and lay lots, inalienable forever. Let us keep the New World *new*, preserve all the advantages of living in the country. There is meadow and pasture and wood-lot for the town's poor. Why not a forest and a huckleberry-field for the town's rich? All Walden Wood might have been preserved for our park forever, with Walden in its midst, and the Easterbrooks Country, an unoccupied area of some four square miles, might have been our huckleberry-field. . . . As some give to Harvard College or another institution, why might not another give a forest or huckleberry-field to Concord? A town is an institution which deserves to be remembered. We boast of our system of education, but why stop at schoolmasters and schoolhouses? We are all schoolmasters, and our schoolhouse is the universe. To attend chiefly to the desk or schoolhouse while we neglect the scenery in which it is placed is absurd. If we do not look out we shall find our fine schoolhouse standing in a cow-yard at last.

JOURNAL 1859

## OCTOBER 16

We need the tonic of wildness,—to wade sometimes in marshes where the bittern and the meadow-hen lurk, and hear the booming of the snipe; to smell the whispering sedge where only some wilder and more solitary fowl builds her nest, and the mink crawls with its belly close to the ground. At the same time that we are earnest to explore and learn all things, we require that all things be mysterious and unexplorable, that land and sea be infinitely wild, unsurveyed and unfathomed by us because unfathomable. We can never have enough of

nature. We must be refreshed by the sight of inex-
haustible vigor, vast and titanic features, the sea-coast
with its wrecks, the wilderness with its living and its
decaying trees, the thunder-cloud, and the rain which
lasts three weeks and produces freshets. We need to witness our own limits transgressed, and some life pastur-
ing freely where we never wander.

WALDEN

## OCTOBER 17

What, after all, does the practicalness of life amount to?
The things immediate to be done are very trivial. I could
postpone them all to hear this locust sing. The most glorious fact in my experience is not anything that I have done
or may hope to do, but a transient thought, or vision, or
dream, which I have had. I would give all the wealth of the
world, and all the deeds of all the heroes, for one true
vision. But how can I communicate with the gods who am
a pencil-maker on the earth, and not be insane?

A WEEK ON THE CONCORD & MERRIMACK RIVERS

## OCTOBER 18

In any weather, at any hour of the day or night, I have
been anxious to improve the nick of time, and notch it
on my stick too; to stand on the meeting of two eternities, the past and future, which is precisely the present
moment; to toe that line. You will pardon some obscuri-

ties, for there are more secrets in my trade than in most men's, and yet not voluntarily kept, but inseparable from its very nature. I would gladly tell all that I know about it, and never paint "No Admittance" on my gate. I long ago lost a hound, a bay horse, and a turtle-dove, and am still on their trail. Many are the travellers I have spoken concerning them, describing their tracks and what calls they answered to. I have met one or two who had heard the hound, and the tramp of the horse, and even seen the dove disappear behind a cloud, and they seemed as anxious to recover them as if they had lost them themselves. To anticipate, not the sunrise and the dawn merely, but, if possible, Nature herself! How many mornings, summer and winter, before yet any neighbor was stirring about his business, have I been about mine! No doubt, many of my townsmen have met me returning from this enterprise, farmers starting for Boston in the twilight, or woodchoppers going to their work. It is true, I never assisted the sun materially in his rising, but, doubt not, it was of the last importance only to be present at it.

WALDEN

## OCTOBER 19

If we have thus desecrated ourselves—as who has not?— the remedy will be by wariness and devotion to reconsecrate ourselves, and make once more a fane of the mind. We should treat our minds, that is, ourselves, as innocent and ingenuous children, whose guardians we are, and be careful what objects and what subjects we thrust on their attention. Read not the Times. Read the Eternities. Conventionalities are at length as bad as impurities. Even the facts of science may dust the mind by their dryness, unless they are in a sense effaced each morning, or rather rendered fertile by the dews of fresh and living truth. Knowledge does not come to us by details, but in flashes of light from heaven.

LIFE WITHOUT PRINCIPLE

## OCTOBER 20

I like I take some satisfaction in eating my food, as well as being nourished by it. . . . I enjoy more drinking water at a clear spring than out of a goblet at a gentleman's table. I like best the bread which I have baked, the garment which I have made, the shelter which I have constructed, the fuel which I have gathered. It is always a recommendation to me to know that a man has ever been poor, has been regularly born into this world, knows the language. I require to be assured of certain philosophers that they have once been barefooted, footsore, have eaten a crust because they had nothing better, and know what sweetness resides in it. I have met with some barren accomplished gentlemen who seemed to have been in school all their lives and never had a vacation to live in. Oh, if they could only have been stolen by the Gypsies! and carried far beyond the reach of their guardians! They had better have died in infancy and been buried under the leaves, their lips besmeared with blackberries, and Cock Robin for their sexton.

## OCTOBER 21

I left the woods for as good a reason as I went there. Perhaps it seemed to me that I had several more lives to live, and could not spare any more time for that one. It is remarkable how easily and insensibly we fall into a particular route, and make a beaten track for ourselves. I had not lived there a week before my feet wore a path from my door to the pond-side; and though it is five or six years since I trod it, it is still quite distinct. It is true, I fear, that others may have fallen into it, and so helped to keep it open. The surface of the earth is soft and impressible by the feet of men; and so with the paths which the mind travels. How worn and dusty, then, must be the highways of the world, how deep the ruts of tradition and conformity! I did not wish to take a cabin passage, but rather to go before the mast and on the deck of the world, for there I could best see the moonlight amid the mountains. I do not wish to go below now.

## OCTOBER 22

It seems as if no man ever died in America; for in order to die you must first have lived. I do not believe in the hearses and palls and funerals that they have had. There was no death in the case, because there had been no life; they merely rotted or sloughed off, pretty much as they had rotted or sloughed along. No temple's veil was rent, only a hole dug somewhere. The best of them fairly ran down like a clock. I hear a good many pretend that they are going to die; or that they have died, for aught I know. Nonsense! I'll defy them to do it. They haven't got life enough in them. They'll deliquesce like fungi, and keep a hundred eulogists mopping the spot where they left off. Only a half a dozen or so have died since the world began. . . . Be sure you die. Finish your work. Know when to leave off. Men make a needless ado about taking lives,—capital punishment. Where is there any life to take? You don't know what it means to let the dead bury the dead.

JOURNAL 1859

## OCTOBER 23

We are acquainted with a mere pellicle of the globe on which we live. Most have not delved six feet beneath the surface, nor leaped as many above it. We know not where we are. Beside, we are sound asleep nearly half our time. Yet we esteem ourselves wise, and have an established order on the surface. Truly, we are deep thinkers, we are ambitious spirits! As I stand over the insect crawling amid the pine needles on the forest floor, and endeavoring to conceal itself from my sight, and ask myself why it will cherish those humble thoughts, and hide its head from me who might, perhaps, be its benefactor, and impart to its race some cheering information, I am reminded of the greater Benefactor and Intelligence that stands over me the human insect.

WALDEN

## OCTOBER 24

We hug the earth—how rarely we mount! Methinks we might elevate ourselves a little more. We might climb a tree at least. I found my account in climbing a tree once. It was a tall white pine on the top of a hill, and though I got well pitched I was well paid for it, for I discovered new mountains in the horizon which I had never seen before,—so much more of the earth and the heavens. I might have walked about the foot of the tree for three score years and ten, and yet I certainly should never have seen them. But, above all, I discovered around me,—it was near the end of June, on the ends of the topmost branches only, a few minute and delicate red cone-like blossoms, the fertile flower of the white pine looking heavenward. . . . The pines have developed their delicate blossoms on the highest twigs of the wood every summer for ages, as well over the heads of Nature's red children, as of her white ones. Yet scarcely a farmer or hunter in the land has ever seen them.

WALKING

## OCTOBER 25

I would not have any one adopt *my* mode of living on any account; for, beside that before he has fairly learned it I may have found out another for myself, I desire that there may be as many different persons in the world as possible; but I would have each one be very careful to find out and pursue *his* own way, and not his father's or his mother's or his neighbor's instead. The youth may build or plant or sail, only let him not be hindered from doing that which he tells me he would like to do. It is by a mathematical point only that we are wise, as the sailor or the fugitive slave keeps the polestar in his eye; but that is sufficient guidance for all our life. We may not arrive at our port within a calculable period, but we would preserve the true course.

WALDEN

## OCTOBER 26

We need pray for no higher heaven than the pure senses can furnish, a *purely* sensuous life. Our present senses are but the rudiments of what they are destined to become. We are comparatively deaf and dumb and blind, and without smell or taste or feeling. Every generation makes the discovery, that its divine vigor has been dissipated, and each sense and faculty misapplied and debauched. The ears were made, not for such trivial uses as men are wont to suppose, but to hear celestial sounds. The eyes were not made for such grovelling uses as they are now put to and worn out by, but to behold beauty now invisible. May we not see God? Are we to be put off and amused in this life, as it were with a mere allegory? ... When the common man looks into the sky, which he has not so much profaned, he thinks it less gross than the earth, and with reverence speaks of "the Heavens," but the seer will in the same sense speak of "the Earths," and his Father who is in them. "Did not he that made that which is *within*, make that which is *without* also?" What is it, then, to educate but to develop these divine germs called the senses? . . . But where is the instructed teacher? Where are the *normal* schools?

A WEEK ON THE CONCORD & MERRIMACK RIVERS

## OCTOBER 27

There are some things of which I cannot at once tell whether I have dreamed them or they are real; as if they were just, perchance, establishing, or else losing a real basis in my world. This is especially the case in the early morning hours, when there is a gradual transition from dreams to waking thoughts, from illusions to actualities, as from darkness, or perchance moon and star light, to sunlight. Dreams are real, as is the light of the stars and moon, and theirs is said to be a *dreamy* light. Such early morning thoughts as I speak of occupy a debatable ground between dreams and thoughts. They are a sort of permanent dream in my mind. At least, until we have for some time changed our position from prostrate to erect, and commenced or faced some of the duties of the day, we cannot tell what we have dreamed from what we have actually experienced.

JOURNAL 1857

## OCTOBER 28

For more than five years I maintained myself thus solely by the labor of my hands, and I found that, by working about six weeks in a year, I could meet all the expenses of living. The whole of my winters, as well as most of my summers, I had free and clear for study. . . . In short, I am convinced, both by faith and experience, that to maintain one's self on this earth is not a hardship but a pastime, if we will live simply and wisely; as the pursuits of the simpler nations are still the sports of the more artificial. It is not necessary that a man should earn his living by the sweat of his brow, unless he sweats easier than I do.

WALDEN

## OCTOBER 29

We see mankind generally either (from ignorance or avarice) toiling too hard and becoming mere machines in order to acquire wealth, or perhaps inheriting it or getting it by other accident, having recourse, for relaxation after excessive toil or as a mere relief to their idle ennui, to artificial amusements, rarely elevating and often debasing. I think that men generally are mistaken with regard to amusements. Every one who deserves to be regarded as higher than the brute may be supposed to have an earnest purpose, to accomplish which is the object of his existence, and this is at once his work and his supremest pleasure; and for diversion and relaxation, for suggestion and education and strength, there is offered the never-failing amusement of getting a living,—never-failing, I mean, when temperately indulged in. I know of no such amusement,—so wholesome and in every sense profitable,—for instance, as to spend an hour or two in a day picking some berries or other fruits which will be food for the winter, or collecting driftwood from the river for fuel, or cultivating the few beans or potatoes which I want. Theatres and operas, which intoxicate for a season, are as nothing compared to these pursuits.

JOURNAL 1857

## OCTOBER 30

It is no dream of mine,
To ornament a line;
I cannot come nearer to God and Heaven
Than I live to Walden even.
I am its stony shore,
And the breeze that passes o'er;
In the hollow of my hand
Are its water and its sand,
And its deepest resort
Lies highest in my thought.

WALDEN

## OCTOBER 31

Looking through a stately pine grove, I saw the western sun falling in golden streams through its aisles. Its west side, opposite to me, was all lit up with golden light; but what was I to it? Such sights remind me of houses which we never inhabit,—that commonly I am not at home in the world. I see somewhat fairer than I enjoy or possess. A fair afternoon, a celestial afternoon, cannot occur but what we mar our pleasure by reproaching ourselves that we do not make all our days beautiful. The thought of what I am, of my pitiful conduct, deters me from receiving what joy I might from the glorious days that visit me. After the era of youth is passed, the knowledge of ourselves is an alloy that spoils our satisfactions. I am wont to think that I could spend my days contentedly in any retired country house that I see; for I see it to advantage now and without incumbrance; I have not yet imported my humdrum thoughts, my prosaic habits, into it to mar the landscape. What is this beauty in the landscape but a certain fertility in me? I look in vain to see it realized but in my own life. If I could wholly cease to be ashamed of myself, I think that all my days would be fair.

NOVEMBER

## NOVEMBER 1

Every morning was a cheerful invitation to make my life of equal simplicity, and I may say innocence, with Nature herself. I have been as sincere a worshipper of Aurora as the Greeks. I got up early and bathed in the pond; that was a religious exercise, and one of the best things which I did. They say that characters were engraven on the bathing tub of king Tching-thang to this effect: "Renew thyself completely each day; do it again, and again, and forever again." I can understand that. Morning brings back the heroic ages. I was as much affected by the faint hum of a mosquito making its invisible and unimaginable tour through my apartment at earliest dawn, when I was sitting with door and windows open, as I could be by any trumpet that ever sang of fame. It was Homer's requiem; itself an Iliad and Odyssey in the air, singing its own wrath and wanderings. There was something cosmical about it; a standing advertisement, till forbidden, of the everlasting vigor and fertility of the world.

WALDEN

## NOVEMBER 2

I believe that there is an ideal or real nature, infinitely more perfect than the actual as there is an ideal life of man. Else where are the glorious summers which in vision sometimes visit my brain? When nature ceases to be supernatural to a man—what will he do then? Of what worth is human life if its actions are no longer to have this sublime and unexplored scenery? Who will build a cottage and dwell in it with enthusiasm if not in the elysian fields?

## NOVEMBER 3

I think that we may safely trust a good deal more than we do. We may waive just so much care of ourselves as we honestly bestow elsewhere. Nature is as well adapted to our weakness as to our strength. The incessant anxiety and strain of some is a well-nigh incurable form of disease. We are made to exaggerate the importance of what work we do; and yet how much is not done by us! or, what if we had been taken sick? How vigilant we are! determined not to live by faith if we can avoid it; all the day long on the alert, at night we unwillingly say our prayers and commit ourselves to uncertainties. So thoroughly and sincerely are we compelled to live, reverencing our life, and denying the possibility of change. This is the only way, we say; but there are as many ways as there can be drawn radii from one centre. All change is a miracle to contemplate; but it is a miracle which is taking place every instant. Confucius said, "To know that we know what we know, and that we do not know what we do not know, that is true knowledge." When one man has reduced a fact of the imagination to be a fact to his understanding, I foresee that all men will at length establish their lives on that basis.

## NOVEMBER 4

We had a remarkable sunset one day last November. I was walking in a meadow, the source of a small brook, when the sun at last, just before setting, after a cold grey day, reached a clear stratum in the horizon, and the softest brightest morning sun-light fell on the dry grass and on the stems of the trees in the opposite horizon, and on the leaves of the shrub-oaks on the hill-side, while our shadows stretched long over the meadow eastward, as if we were the only motes in its beams. It was such a light as we could not have imagined a moment before, and the air also was so warm and serene that nothing was wanting to make a paradise of that meadow. When we reflected that this was not a solitary phenomenon, never to happen again, but that it would happen forever and ever an infinite number of evenings, and cheer and reassure the latest child that walked there, it was more glorious still.

WALKING

## NOVEMBER 5

I should relish getting my living in a simple, primitive fashion. The life which society proposes to me to live is so artificial and complex—bolstered up on many weak supports, and sure to topple down at last—that no man surely can ever be inspired to live it, and only "old fogies" ever praise it. At best some think it their duty to live it. I believe in the infinite joy and satisfaction of helping myself and others to the extent of my ability. But is the use in trying to live simply, raising what you eat, making what you wear, building what you inhabit, burning what you cut or dig, when those to whom you are allied insanely want and will have a thousand other things which neither you nor they can raise and nobody else, perchance, will pay for?

## NOVEMBER 6

The student who secures his coveted leisure and retirement by systematically shirking any labor necessary to man obtains but an ignoble and unprofitable leisure, defrauding himself of the experience which alone can make leisure fruitful. . . . I mean that they should not *play* life, or *study* it merely, while the community supports them at this expensive game, but earnestly *live* it from beginning to end. How could youths better learn to live than by at once trying the experiment of living? Methinks this would exercise their minds as much as mathematics. If I wished a boy to know something about the arts and sciences, for instance, I would not pursue the common course, which is merely to send him into the neighborhood of some professor, where anything is professed and practised but the art of life;—survey the world through a telescope or a microscope, and never with his natural eye; to study chemistry, and not learn how his bread is made, or mechanics, and not learn how it is earned; to discover new satellites to Neptune, and not detect the motes in his eyes, or to what vagabond he is a satellite himself; or to be devoured by the monsters that swarm all around him, while contemplating the monsters in a drop of vinegar. . . . Even the *poor* student studies and is taught only *political* economy, while that economy of living which is synonymous with philosophy is not even sincerely professed in our colleges.

WALDEN

## NOVEMBER 7

Cast your whole vote, not a strip of paper merely, but your whole influence. A minority is powerless while it conforms to the majority; it is not even a minority then; but it is irresistible when it clogs by its whole weight. If the alternative is to keep all just men in prison, or give up war and slavery, the State will not hesitate which to choose. If a thousand men were not to pay their tax-bills this year, that would not be a violent and bloody measure, as it would be to pay them, and enable the State to commit violence and shed innocent blood. This is, in fact, the definition of a peaceable revolution, if any such is possible.

RESISTANCE TO CIVIL GOVERNMENT

## NOVEMBER 8

I, too, would fain set down something beside facts. Facts should only be as the frame to my pictures; they should be material to the mythology which I am writing; not facts to assist men to make money, farmers to farm profitably, in any common sense; facts to tell who I am, and

where I have been or what I have thought: as now the
bell rings for evening meeting, and its volumes of sound,
like smoke which rises from where a cannon is fired,
make the tent in which I dwell. My facts all be falsehoods
to the common sense. I would so state facts that they
shall be significant, shall be myths or mythologic. Facts
which the mind perceived, thoughts which the body
thought,—with these I deal.

JOURNAL 1851

## NOVEMBER 9

We are wont to forget that the sun looks on our cultivated
fields and on the prairies and forests without distinction.
They all reflect and absorb his rays alike, and the former
make but a small part of the glorious picture which he
beholds in his daily course. In his view the earth is all
equally cultivated like a garden. Therefore we should
receive the benefit of his light and heat with a corresponding trust and magnanimity. What though I value
the seed of these beans, and harvest that in the fall of the
year? This broad field which I have looked at so long
looks not to me as the principal cultivator, but away
from me to influences more genial to it, which water and
make it green. These beans have results which are not
harvested by me. Do they not grow for woodchucks
partly? . . . Shall I not rejoice also at the abundance of the
weeds whose seeds are the granary of the birds? It matters little comparatively whether the fields fill the

farmer's barns. The true husbandman will cease from anxiety, as the squirrels manifest no concern whether the woods will bear chestnuts this year or not, and finish his labor with every day, relinquishing all claim to the produce of his fields, and sacrificing in his mind not only his first but his last fruits also.

WALDEN

## NOVEMBER 10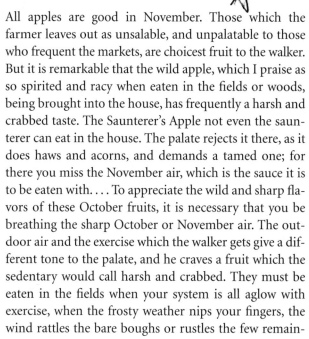

All apples are good in November. Those which the farmer leaves out as unsalable, and unpalatable to those who frequent the markets, are choicest fruit to the walker. But it is remarkable that the wild apple, which I praise as so spirited and racy when eaten in the fields or woods, being brought into the house, has frequently a harsh and crabbed taste. The Saunterer's Apple not even the saunterer can eat in the house. The palate rejects it there, as it does haws and acorns, and demands a tamed one; for there you miss the November air, which is the sauce it is to be eaten with. . . . To appreciate the wild and sharp flavors of these October fruits, it is necessary that you be breathing the sharp October or November air. The outdoor air and the exercise which the walker gets give a different tone to the palate, and he craves a fruit which the sedentary would call harsh and crabbed. They must be eaten in the fields when your system is all aglow with exercise, when the frosty weather nips your fingers, the wind rattles the bare boughs or rustles the few remaining leaves, and the jay is heard screaming around. What is sour in the house a bracing walk makes sweet. Some of these apples might be labeled, "To be eaten in the wind."

WILD APPLES

## NOVEMBER 11

It is remarkable that the highest intellectual mood which the world tolerates is the perception of the truth of the most ancient revelations, now in some respects out of date; but any direct revelation, any original thoughts, it hates like virtue. The fathers and the mothers of this town would rather hear the young man or young woman at their tables express reverence for some old statement of the truth than utter a direct revelation themselves. . . . So far as thinking is concerned, surely original thinking is the divinest thing. Rather we should reverently watch for the least motions, the least scintillations, of thought in this sluggish world, and men should run to and fro on the occasion more than at an earthquake. We check and repress the divinity that stirs within us, to fall down and worship the divinity that is dead without us. I go to see many a good man or good woman, so called, and utter freely that thought which alone it was given me to utter; but there was a man who lived a long, long time ago, and his name was Moses, and another whose name was Christ, and if your thought does not, or does not appear to, coincide with what they said, the good man or good woman has no ears to hear you. They think they love God! It is only his old clothes, of which they make scarecrows for the children. Where will they come nearer to God than in those very children?

JOURNAL 1851

## NOVEMBER 12

I cannot help feeling that of all the human inhabitants of nature hereabouts, only we two have leisure to admire and enjoy our inheritance. "Free in this world, as the birds in the air, disengaged from every kind of chains, those who have practiced the *yoga* gather in Brahma the certain fruit of their works." Depend upon it that rude and careless as I am, I would fain practise the *yoga* faithfully. . . . To some extent, and at rare intervals, even I am a yogi.

LETTERS 1849

## NOVEMBER 13

What is the pill which will keep us well, serene, contented? Not my or thy great-grandfather's, but our great-grandmother Nature's universal, vegetable, botanic medicines, by which she has kept herself young always, outlived so many old Parrs in her day, and fed her health with their decaying fatness. For my panacea, instead of one of those quack vials of a mixture dipped from Acheron and the Dead Sea, which come out of those long shallow black-schooner looking wagons which we sometimes see made to carry bottles, let me have a draught of undiluted morning air. Morning air! If men will not drink of this at the fountainhead of the day, why, then, we must even bottle up some and sell it in the shops, for the benefit of those who have lost their subscription ticket to morning time in this world.

WALDEN

## NOVEMBER 14

There is nowhere any apology for despondency. Always there is life which, rightly lived, implies a divine satisfaction. I am soothed by the rain-drops on the door-sill; every globule that pitches thus confidently from the eves to the ground is my life insurance. Disease and a rain-drop cannot coexist. The east wind is not itself consumptive, but has enjoyed a rare health from of old. If a fork or brand stand erect, *good* is portended by it. They are the warrant of universal innocence.

JOURNAL 1839

## NOVEMBER 15

Let me see; where was I? Methinks I was nearly in this frame of mind; the world lay about at this angle. Shall I go to heaven or a-fishing? If I should soon bring this meditation to an end, would another so sweet an occasion be likely to offer? I was as near being resolved into the essence of things as ever I was in my life. I fear my thoughts will not come back to me. If it would do any good, I would whistle for them. When they make us an offer, is it wise to say, We will think of it? My thoughts have left no track, and I cannot find the path again. What was it that I was thinking of? It was a very hazy day. I will just try these three sentences of Con-fut-see; they may fetch that state about again. I know not whether it was the dumps or a budding ecstasy. Mem. There never is but one opportunity of a kind.

## NOVEMBER 16

My Journal should be the record of my love. I would write in it only of the things I love, my affection for any aspect of the world, what I love to think of. I have no more distinctness or pointedness in my yearnings than an expanding bud, which does indeed point to flower and fruit, to summer and autumn, but is aware of the warm sun and spring influence only. I feel ripe for something, yet do nothing, can't discover what that thing is. I feel fertile merely. It is seedtime with me. I have lain fallow long enough. Notwithstanding a sense of unworthiness which possesses me, not without reason, notwithstanding that I regard myself as a good deal of a scamp, yet for the most part the spirit of the universe is unaccountably kind to me, and I enjoy perhaps an unusual share of happiness. Yet I question sometimes if there is not some settlement to come.

## NOVEMBER 17

The merchants and company have long laughed at transcendentalism, higher laws, etc., crying, "None of your moonshine," as if they were anchored to something not only definite, but sure and permanent. If there was any institution which was presumed to rest on a solid and secure basis, and more than any other represented this boasted common sense, prudence, and practical talent, it was the bank; and now those very banks are found to be mere reeds shaken by the wind. Scarcely one in the land has kept its promise. . . . Hard times, I say, have this value, among others, that they show us what such promises are worth,—where the *sure* banks are.

LETTERS 1857


## NOVEMBER 18

What is it that makes it so hard sometimes to determine whither we will walk? I believe that there is a subtile magnetism in Nature, which, if we unconsciously yield to it, will direct us aright. It is not indifferent to us which way we walk. There is a right way; but we are very liable from heedlessness and stupidity to take the wrong one. We would fain take that walk, never yet taken by us through this actual world, which is perfectly symbolical of the path which we love to travel in the interior and ideal world; and sometimes, no doubt, we find it difficult to choose our direction, because it does not yet exist distinctly in our idea.

WALKING

## NOVEMBER 19

The time must come when this coast will be a place of resort for those New-Englanders who really wish to visit the sea-side. At present it is wholly unknown to the fashionable world, and probably it will never be agreeable to them. . . . But this shore will never be more attractive than it is now. Such beaches as are fashionable are here made and unmade in a day, I may almost say, by the sea shifting its sands. Lynn and Nantasket! this bare and bended arm it is that makes the bay in which they lie so snugly. What are springs and waterfalls? Here is the spring of springs, the waterfall of waterfalls. A storm in the fall or winter is the time to visit it; a light-house or a fisherman's hut the true hotel. A man may stand there and put all America behind him.

CAPE COD

## NOVEMBER 20

A man is worth most to himself and to others, whether as an observer, or poet, or neighbor or friend, where he is most himself, most contented and at home. There his life is the most intense and he loses the fewest moments. Familiar and surrounding objects are the best symbols and illustrations of his life. If a man who has had deep experiences should endeavor to describe them in a book of travels, it would be to use the language of a wandering tribe instead of a universal language. The poet has made the best roots in his native soil of any man, and is the hardest to transplant. The man who is often thinking that it is better to be somewhere else than where he is excommunicates himself. If a man is rich and strong anywhere, it must be on his native soil. Here I have been these forty years learning the language of these fields that I may the better express myself. If I should travel to the prairies, I should much less understand them, and my past life would serve me but ill to describe them. Many a weed here stands for more of life to me than the big trees of California would if I should go there. We only need travel enough to give our intellects an airing. In spite of Malthus and the rest, there will be plenty of room in this world, if every man will mind his own business. I have not heard of any planet running against another yet.

JOURNAL 1857

 ## NOVEMBER 21

I went to the woods because I wished to live deliberately, to front only the essential facts of life, and see if I could not learn what it had to teach, and not, when I came to die, discover that I had not lived. I did not wish to live what was not life, living is so dear; nor did I wish to practise resignation, unless it was quite necessary. I wanted to live deep and suck out all the marrow of life, to live so sturdily and Spartan-like as to put to rout all that was not life, to cut a broad swath and shave close, to drive life into a corner, and reduce it to its lowest terms, and, if it proved to be mean, why then to get the whole and genuine meanness of it, and publish its meanness to the world; or if it were sublime, to know it by experience, and be able to give a true account of it in my next excursion. For most men, it appears to me, are in a strange uncertainty about it, whether it is of the devil or of God, and have *somewhat hastily* concluded that it is the chief end of man here to "glorify God and enjoy him forever."

WALDEN

## NOVEMBER 22

You must have been enriched by your solitary walk over the mountains. I suppose that I feel the same awe when on their summits that many do on entering a church. To see what kind of earth that is on which you have a house and garden somewhere, perchance! It is equal to the lapse of many years. You must ascend a mountain to learn your relation to matter, and so to your own body, for *it* is at home there, though *you* are not. It might have been composed there, and will have no further to go to return to dust there, than in your garden; but your spirit inevitably comes away, and brings your body with it, if it lives. Just as awful really, and as glorious, is your garden.

LETTERS 1857

## NOVEMBER 23

My days were not days of the week, bearing the stamp of any heathen deity, nor were they minced into hours and fretted by the ticking of a clock; for I lived like the Puri

Indians, of whom it is said that "for yesterday, to-day, and to-morrow they have only one word, and they express the variety of meaning by pointing backward for yesterday, forward for to-morrow, and overhead for the passing day." This was sheer idleness to my fellow-townsmen, no doubt; but if the birds and flowers had tried me by their standard, I should not have been found wanting. A man must find his occasions in himself, it is true. The natural day is very calm, and will hardly reprove his indolence.

WALDEN

## NOVEMBER 24

It would be a relief to breathe one's self occasionally among men. If there were any magnanimity in us, any grandeur of soul, anything but sects and parties under-taking to patronize God and keep the mind within bounds, how often we might encourage and provoke one another by a free expression! I will not consent to walk with my mouth muzzled. . . . Freedom of speech! It hath not entered into your hearts to conceive what those words mean. It is not leave given me by your sect to say this or that; it is when leave is given to your sect to with-draw. The church, the state, the school, the magazine, think they are liberal and free! It is the freedom of a prison-yard. . . . Let us have institutions framed not out of our rottenness, but out of our soundness. This facti-tious piety is like stale gingerbread. I would like to sug-gest what a pack of fools and cowards we mankind are.

They want me to agree not to breathe too hard in the neighborhood of their paper castles. If I should draw a long breath in the neighborhood of these institutions, their weak and flabby sides would fall out, for my own inspiration would exhaust the air about them.

JOURNAL 1858

## NOVEMBER 25

If I were confined to a corner of a garret all my days, like a spider, the world would be just as large to me while I had my thoughts about me. . . . We are often reminded that if there were bestowed on us the wealth of Croesus, our aims must still be the same, and our means essentially the same. Moreover, if you are restricted in your range by poverty, if you cannot buy books and newspapers, for instance, you are but confined to the most significant and vital experiences; you are compelled to deal with the material which yields the most sugar and the most starch. It is life near the bone where it is sweetest. You are defended from being a trifler. No man loses ever on a lower level by magnanimity on a higher. Superfluous wealth can buy superfluities only. Money is not required to buy one necessary of the soul.

WALDEN

## NOVEMBER 26

It is something to know when you are addressed by Divinity and not by a common traveller. I went down cellar just now to get an armful of wood and, passing the brick piers with my wood and candle, I heard, methought, a commonplace suggestion, but when, as it were by accident, I reverently attended to the hint, I found that it was the voice of a god who had followed me down cellar to speak to me. How many communications may we not lose through inattention! I would fain keep a journal which should contain those thoughts and impressions which I am most liable to forget that I have had; which would have in one sense the greatest remoteness, in another, the greatest nearness to me. 'Tis healthy to be sick sometimes.

JOURNAL 1851

## NOVEMBER 27

My desire for knowledge is intermittent; but my desire to bathe my head in atmospheres unknown to my feet is perennial and constant. The highest that we can attain to is not Knowledge, but Sympathy with Intelligence. I do not know that this higher knowledge amounts to anything more definite than a novel and grand surprise on a sudden revelation of the insufficiency of all that we called Knowledge before,—a discovery that there are more things in heaven and earth than are dreamed of in our philosophy. It is the lighting up of the mist by the sun. Man cannot know in any higher sense than this, any more than he can look serenely and with impunity in the face of the sun.

WALKING

## NOVEMBER 28

Let us spend one day as deliberately as Nature, and not be thrown off the track by every nutshell and mosquito's wing that falls on the rails. Let us rise early and fast, or break fast, gently and without perturbation; let company come and let company go, let the bells ring and the children cry,—determined to make a day of it. Why should we knock under and go with the stream? Let us not be upset and overwhelmed in that terrible rapid and whirlpool called a dinner, situated in the meridian shallows. Weather this danger and you are safe, for the rest of the way is down hill. With unrelaxed nerves, with morning vigor, sail by it, looking another way, tied to the mast like Ulysses. If the engine whistles, let it whistle till it is hoarse for its pains. If the bell rings, why should we run? We will consider what kind of music they are like.

WALDEN

## NOVEMBER 29

The title *wise* is, for the most part, falsely applied. How can one be a wise man, if he does not know any better how to live than other men?—if he is only more cunning and intellectually subtle? Does Wisdom work in a treadmill? or does she teach how to succeed *by her example*? Is there any such thing as wisdom not applied to life? Is she merely the miller who grinds the finest logic? It is pertinent to ask if Plato got his *living* in a better way or more successfully than his contemporaries,—or did he succumb to the difficulties of life like other men? Did he seem to prevail over some of them merely by indifference, or by assuming grand airs? or find it easier to live, because his aunt remembered him in her will? The ways in which most men get their living, that is, live, are mere make-shifts, and a shirking of the real business of life,— chiefly because they do not know, but partly because they do not mean, any better.

LIFE WITHOUT PRINCIPLE

## NOVEMBER 30

Nothing is so attractive and unceasingly curious as character. There is no plant that needs such tender treatment, there is none that will endure so rough. It is the violet and the oak. It is the thing we mean, let us say what we will. We mean our own character, or we mean yours. It is divine and related to the heavens, as the earth is by the flashes of the Aurora. It has no acquaintance nor companion. It goes silent and unobserved longer than any planet in space, but when at length it does show itself, it seems like the flowering of all the world, and its before unseen orbit is lit up like the trail of a meteor. I hear no good news ever but some trait of a noble character.

JOURNAL 1841

DECEMBER

## DECEMBER 1

Let us settle ourselves, and work and wedge our feet downward through the mud and slush of opinion, and prejudice, and tradition, and delusion, and appearance, that alluvion which covers the globe, through Paris and London, through New York and Boston and Concord, through church and state, through poetry and philosophy and religion, till we come to a hard bottom and rocks in place, which we can call reality, and say, This is, and no mistake; and then begin, having a *point d'appui*, below freshet and frost and fire, a place where you might found a wall or a state, or set a lamp-post safely, or perhaps a gauge, not a Nilometer, but a Realometer, that future ages might know how deep a freshet of shams and appearances had gathered from time to time. If you stand right fronting and face to face to a fact, you will see the sun glimmer on both its surfaces, as if it were a cimeter, and feel its sweet edge dividing you through the heart and marrow, and so you will happily conclude your mortal career. Be it life or death, we crave only reality. If we are really dying, let us hear the rattle in our throats and feel cold in the extremities; if we are alive, let us go about our business.

WALDEN

## DECEMBER 2

I sailed up a river with a pleasant wind,
New lands, new people, and new thoughts to find;

Many fair reaches and headlands appeared,
And many dangers were there to be feared;
But when I remember where I have been,
And the fair landscapes that I have seen,
THOU seemest the only permanent shore,
The cape never rounded, nor wandered o'er.

A WEEK ON THE CONCORD & MERRIMACK RIVERS

## DECEMBER 3

That age will be rich indeed when those relics which we call Classics, and the still older and more than classic but even less known Scriptures of the nations, shall have still further accumulated, when the Vaticans shall be filled with Vedas and Zendavestas and Bibles, with Homers and Dantes and Shakespeares, and all the centuries to come shall have successively deposited their trophies in the forum of the world. By such a pile we may hope to scale heaven at last. The works of the great poets have never yet been read by mankind, for only the great poets can read them. They have only been read as the multitude read the stars, at most astrologically, not astronomically. Most men have learned to read to serve a paltry convenience, as they have learned to cipher in order to keep accounts and not be cheated in trade; but of reading as a noble intellectual exercise they know little or nothing; yet this only is reading, in a high sense, not that which lulls us as a luxury and suffers the nobler faculties to sleep the while, but what we have to stand on tiptoe to read and devote our most alert and wakeful hours to.

WALDEN

## DECEMBER 4

Let youth seize upon the finest and most memorable experience in their lives—that which most reconciled them to their unknown destiny—and seek to discover in it their future path. Let them be sure that that way is their only true and worthy career. All mortals sent into this world have a star in the heavens appointed to guide them. Its ray they cannot mistake. It has sent its beam to them either through clouds and mists faintly or through a serene heaven. They know better than to seek the advice of any. Of how much improvement are we susceptible—and what are the methods?

JOURNAL 1846

## DECEMBER 5

True, a man cannot lift himself by his own waistbands, because he cannot get out of himself; but he can expand himself (which is better, there being no up nor down in nature), and so split his waistbands, being already within himself. You speak of doing and being, and the vanity, real or apparent, of much doing. . . . The other day I opened a muskrat's house. It was made of weeds, five feet broad at base, and three feet high, and far and low within it was a little cavity, only a foot in diameter, where the rat dwelt. It may seem trivial, this piling up of weeds, but so the race of muskrats is preserved. We must heap up a great pile of doing, for a small diameter of being.

LETTERS 1853

## DECEMBER 6

The cost of a thing is the amount of what I will call life which is required to be exchanged for it, immediately or in the long run. An average house in this neighborhood costs perhaps eight hundred dollars, and to lay up this sum will take from ten to fifteen years of the laborer's life, even if he is not encumbered with a family;—estimating the pecuniary value of every man's labor at one dollar a day, for if some receive more, others receive less;—so that he must have spent more than half his life commonly before his wigwam will be earned. If we suppose him to pay a rent instead, this is but a doubtful choice of evils.

WALDEN

## DECEMBER 7

I can easily walk ten, fifteen, twenty, any number of miles, commencing at my own door, without going by any house, without crossing a road except where the fox and the mink do: First along by the river, and then the brook, and then the meadow and the wood-side. There are square miles in my vicinity which have no inhabitant.

From many a hill I can see civilization and the abodes of man afar. The farmers and their works are scarcely more obvious than woodchucks and their burrows. Man and his affairs, church and state—and school, trade and commerce, and manufactures and agriculture, —even politics, the most alarming of them all,—I am pleased to see how little space they occupy in the landscape.

WALKING

## DECEMBER 8

Winter has come unnoticed by me, I have been so busy writing. This is the life most lead in respect to Nature. How different from my habitual one! It is hasty, coarse, and trivial, as if you were a spindle in a factory. The other is leisurely, fine, and glorious, like a flower. In the first case you are merely getting your living; in the second you live as you go along. You travel only on roads of the proper grade without jar or running off the track, and sweep round the hills by beautiful curves. Went over the fields on the crust to Walden, over side of Bear Garden. Already foxes have left their tracks. How the crust shines afar, the sun now setting! There is a glorious clear sunset sky, soft and delicate and warm even like a pigeon's neck. Why do the mountains never look so fair as from my native fields?

JOURNAL 1854

## DECEMBER 9

We discourse freely without shame of one form of sensuality, and are silent about another. We are so degraded that we cannot speak simply of the necessary functions of human nature. In earlier ages, in some countries, every function was reverently spoken of and regulated by law. Nothing was too trivial for the Hindoo lawgiver, however offensive it may be to modern taste. He teaches how to eat, drink, cohabit, void excrement and urine, and the like, elevating what is mean, and does not falsely excuse himself by calling these things trifles. Every man is the builder of a temple, called his body, to the god he worships, after a style purely his own, nor can he get off by hammering marble instead. We are all sculptors and painters, and our material is our own flesh and blood and bones. Any nobleness begins at once to refine a man's features, any meanness or sensuality to imbrute them.

WALDEN

## DECEMBER 10

In short, all good things are wild and free. There is something in a strain of music, whether produced by an instrument or by the human voice,—take the sound of a bugle in a summer night, for instance,—which by its wildness, to speak without satire, reminds me of the cries emitted by wild beasts in their native forests. It is so much of their wildness as I can understand. Give me for my friends and neighbors wild men, not tame ones. The

wildness of the savage is but a faint symbol of the awful
ferity with which good men and lovers meet.

WALKING


## DECEMBER 11

My body is all sentient. As I go here or there, I am tickled
by this or that I come in contact with, as if I touched the
wires of a battery. . . . The age of miracles is each moment
thus returned. Now it is wild apples, now river reflec-
tions, now a flock of lesser redpolls. In winter, too, resides
immortal youth and perennial summer. Its head is not
silvered; its cheek is not blanched but has a ruby tinge to
it. If any part of nature excites our pity, it is for ourselves
we grieve, for there is eternal health and beauty. We get
only transient and partial glimpses of the beauty of the
world. Standing at the right angle, we are dazzled by the
colors of the rainbow in colorless ice. From the right
point of view, every storm and every drop in it is a rainbow. Beauty and music are not mere traits and excep-
tions. They are the rule and character. It is the exception
that we see and hear. Then I try to discover what it was in
the vision that charmed and translated me. What if we
could daguerrotype our thoughts and feelings! for I am
surprised and enchanted often by some quality which I
cannot detect. I have seen an attribute of another world
and condition of things. It is a wonderful fact that I
should be affected, and thus deeply and powerfully, more
than by aught else in all my experience,—that this fruit

should be borne in me, sprung from a seed finer than the spores of fungi, floated from other atmospheres! finer than the dust caught in the sails of vessels a thousand miles from land! Here the invisible seeds settle, and spring, and bear flowers and fruits of immortal beauty.

JOURNAL 1855

## DECEMBER 12

I have been surveying for twenty or thirty days, living coarsely, even as respects my diet,—for I find that that will always alter to suit my employment,—indeed, leading a quite trivial life; and to-night, for the first time, had made a fire in my chamber and endeavored to return to myself. I wished to ally myself to the powers that rule the universe. I wished to dive into some deep stream of thoughtful and devoted life, which meandered through retired and fertile meadows far from towns. I wished to do again, or for once, things quite congenial to my highest inmost and most sacred nature, to lurk in crystalline thought like the trout under verdurous banks, where stray mankind should only see my bubble come to the surface. I wished to live, ah! as far away as a man can think. I wished for leisure and quiet to let my life flow in its proper channels, with its proper currents, when I might not waste the days, might establish daily prayer and thanksgiving in my family; might do my own work and not the work of Concord and Carlisle, which would yield me better than money.

JOURNAL 1851

## DECEMBER 13

If you are going into that line,—going to besiege the city of God,—you must not only be strong in engines, but prepared with provisions to starve out the garrison. An Irishman came to see me to-day, who is endeavoring to get his family out to this New World. He rises at half past four, milks twenty-eight cows (which has swollen the joints of his fingers), and eats his breakfast, without any milk in his tea or coffee, before six; and so on, day after day, for six and a half dollars a month; and thus he keeps his virtue in him, if he does not add to it; and he regards me as a gentleman able to assist him; but if I ever get to be a gentleman, it will be by working after my fashion harder than he does. If my joints are not swollen, it must be because I deal with the teats of celestial cows before breakfast (and the milker in this case is always allowed some of the milk for his breakfast), to say nothing of the flocks and herds of Admetus afterward. It is the art of mankind to polish the world, and everyone who works is scrubbing in some part.

LETTERS 1853

## DECEMBER 14

There is a solid bottom everywhere. We read that the traveller asked the boy if the swamp before him had a hard bottom. The boy replied that it had. But presently the traveller's horse sank in up to the girths, and he observed to the boy, "I thought you said that this bog had a hard bottom." "So it has," answered the latter, "but you have not got half way to it yet." So it is with the bogs and quicksands of society. . . . I would not be one of those who will foolishly drive a nail into mere lath and plastering; such a deed would keep me awake nights. Give me a hammer, and let me feel for the furring. Do not depend on the putty. Drive a nail home and clinch it so faithfully that you can wake up in the night and think of your work with satisfaction,—a work at which you would not be ashamed to invoke the Muse. So will help you God, and so only. Every nail driven should be as another rivet in the machine of the universe, you carrying on the work.

WALDEN


## DECEMBER 15

The ways by which you may get money almost without exception lead downward. To have done anything by which you earned money *merely* is to have been truly idle or worse. If the laborer gets no more than the wages which his employer pays him, he is cheated, he cheats himself. If you would get money as a writer or lecturer, you must be popular, which is to go down perpendicularly. Those services which the community will most readily pay for, it is most disagreeable to render. You are paid for being something less than a man.

LIFE WITHOUT PRINCIPLE

## DECEMBER 16

The wisest man preaches no doctrines; he has no scheme; he sees no rafter, not even a cobweb, against the heavens. It is clear sky. If I ever see more clearly at one time than at another, the medium through which I see is clearer. To see from earth to heaven, and see there standing, still a fixture. . . . What right have you to hold up this obstacle to my understanding you, to your understanding me! You did not invent it; it was imposed on you. Examine your authority. Even Christ, we fear, had his scheme, his conformity to tradition, which slightly vitiates his teaching. He had not swallowed all formulas. He preached some mere doctrines.

A WEEK ON THE CONCORD & MERRIMACK RIVERS

## DECEMBER 17

I see young men, my townsmen, whose misfortune it is to have inherited farms, houses, barns, cattle, and farming tools; for these are more easily acquired than got rid of. Better if they had been born in the open pasture and suckled by a wolf, that they might have seen with clearer eyes what field they were called to labor in. Who made them serfs of the soil? Why should they eat their sixty acres, when man is condemned to eat only his peck of dirt? Why should they begin digging their graves as soon as they are born? They have got to live a man's life, pushing all these things before them, and get on as well as they can. How many a poor immortal soul have I met

well-nigh crushed and smothered under its load, creep-
ing down the road of life, pushing before it a barn
seventy-five feet by forty, its Augean stables never
cleansed, and one hundred acres of land, tillage, mow-
ing, pasture, and woodlot!

WALDEN

## DECEMBER 18

I would fain write to you now by broad daylight, and
report to you some of my life, such as it is, and recall you
to your life, which is not always lived by you, even by day
light. Blake! Blake! Are you awake? Are you aware what
an ever-glorious morning this is,—what long expected
never to be repeated opportunity is now offered to get
life and knowledge? For my part I am trying to wake
up,—to wring slumber out of my pores; —for, generally,
I take events as unconcernedly as a fence-post,—absorb
wet and cold like it, and am pleasantly tickled with
lichens slowly spreading over me.

LETTERS  1856

## DECEMBER 19

No man ever stood the lower in my estimation for having a patch in his clothes; yet I am sure that there is
greater anxiety, commonly, to have fashionable, or at
least clean and unpatched clothes, than to have a sound
conscience. . . . Who could wear a patch, or two extra
seams only, over the knee? Most behave as if they

believed their prospects for life would be ruined if they should do it. It would be easier for them to hobble to town with a broken leg than with a broken pantaloon. Often if an accident happens to a gentleman's legs, they can be mended; but if a similar accident happens to the legs of his pantaloons, there is no help for it; for he considers, not what is truly respectable, but what is respected. We know but few men, a great many coats and breeches. . . . It is an interesting question how far men would retain their relative rank if they were divested of their clothes.

WALDEN

## DECEMBER 20

Dreams are the touchstones of our characters. We are scarcely less afflicted when we remember some unworthiness in our conduct in a dream, than if it had been actual, and the intensity of our grief, which is our atonement, measures the degree by which this is separated from an actual unworthiness. For in dreams we but act a part which must have been learned and rehearsed in our waking hours, and no doubt could discover some waking consent thereto. If this meanness had not its foundation in us, why are we grieved at it? In dreams we see ourselves naked and acting out our real characters, even more clearly than we see others awake. But an unwavering and commanding virtue would compel even its most fantastic and faintest dreams to respect its ever-wakeful authority; as we are accustomed to say carelessly, we should never have dreamed of such a thing. Our truest life is when we are in dreams awake.

A WEEK ON THE CONCORD & MERRIMACK RIVERS

## DECEMBER 21

In the fields only are the sours and bitters of Nature appreciated; just as the wood-chopper eats his meal in a sunny glade, in the middle of a winter day, with content, basks in a sunny ray there and dreams of summer in a degree of cold which, experienced in a chamber, would make a student miserable. . . . As with temperatures, so with flavors; as with cold and heat, so with sour and sweet. This natural raciness, the sours and bitters which the diseased palate refuses, are the true condiments. Let your condiments be in the condition of your senses. To appreciate the flavor of these wild apples requires vigorous and healthy senses. . . . What a healthy out-of-door appetite it takes to relish the apple of life, the apple of the world then! . . . So there is one *thought* for the field, another for the house. I would have my thoughts, like wild apples, to be food for walkers, and will not warrant them to be palatable if tasted in the house.

WILD APPLES

## DECEMBER 22

It is worth the while to apply the wisdom one has to the conduct of his life, surely. I find myself oftenest wise in little things and foolish in great ones. That I may accomplish some particular petty affair well, I live my whole life coarsely. A broad margin of leisure is as beautiful in a man's life as in a book. Haste makes waste, no less in life than in housekeeping. Keep the time, observe the hours of the universe, not of the cars. What are three-score years and ten hurriedly and coarsely lived to moments of divine leisure in which your life is coincident with the life of the universe? We live too fast and coarsely, just as we eat too fast, and do not know the true savor of our food. We consult our will and understanding and the expectation of men, not our genius. I can impose upon myself tasks which will crush me for life and prevent all expansion, and this I am but too inclined to do. One moment of life costs many hours, hours not of business but of preparation and invitation. Yet the man who does not betake himself at once and desperately to sawing is called a loafer, though he may be knocking at the doors of heaven all the while, which shall surely be opened to him. That aim in life is highest which requires the highest and finest discipline. How much, what infinite, leisure it requires, as of a lifetime, to appreciate a single phenomenon! You must camp down beside it as for life, having reached your land of promise, and give yourself wholly to it. It must stand for the whole world to you, symbolical of all things.

## DECEMBER 23

I am grateful for what I am and have. My thanksgiving is perpetual. It is surprising how contented one can be with nothing definite—only a sense of existence. . . . O how I laugh when I think of my vague indefinite riches. No run on my bank can drain it—for my wealth is not possession but enjoyment. Whare are all these years made for? And now another winter comes, so much like the last! Can't we satisfy the beggars once for all? Have you got your wood in for this winter? What else have you got in? Of what use a great fire on the hearth and confounded little fire in the heart? Are you prepared to make a decisive campaign—to pay for your costly tuition—to pay for the suns of past summers—for happiness and unhappiness lavished upon you? Does not Time go by swifter than the swiftest equine trotter or racker?

LETTERS 1856

## DECEMBER 24

I want to go soon and live away by the pond, where I shall hear only the wind whispering among the reeds. It will be success if I shall have left myself behind. But my friends ask what I will do when I get there. Will it not be employment enough to watch the progress of the seasons? I don't want to feel as if my life were a sojourn any longer. That philosophy cannot be true which so paints it. It is time now that I begin to live.

JOURNAL 1841

## DECEMBER 25

Yet the New Testament treats of man and man's so-called spiritual affairs too exclusively, and is too constantly moral and personal, to alone content me, who am not interested solely in man's religious or moral nature, or in man even. I have not the most definite designs on the future. Absolutely speaking, Do unto others as you would that they should do unto you, is by no means a golden rule, but the best of current silver. An honest man would have but little occasion for it. It is golden not to have any rule at all in such a case. The book has never been written which is to be accepted without any allowance. Christ was a sublime actor on the stage of the world. He knew what he was thinking of when he said, "Heaven and earth shall pass away, but my words shall not pass away." I draw near to him at such a time. Yet he taught mankind but imperfectly how to live; his thoughts were all directed toward another world. There is another kind of success than his. Even here we have a sort of living to get, and must buffet it somewhat longer. There are various tough problems yet to solve, and we must make shift to live, betwixt spirit and matter, such a human life as we can.

A WEEK ON THE CONCORD & MERRIMACK RIVERS

## DECEMBER 26

He is the rich man and enjoys the fruits of riches, who, summer and winter forever, can find delight in the contemplation of his soul. I could look as unweariedly up to that cope as into the heavens of a summer day or a winter night. When I hear this bell ring, I am carried back to years and Sabbaths when I was newer and more innocent, I fear, than now, and it seems to me as if there were a world within a world. Sin, I am sure, is not in overt acts or, indeed, in acts of any kind, but is in proportion to the time which has come behind us and displaced eternity,—that degree to which our elements are mixed with the elements of the world. The whole duty of life is contained in the question how to respire and aspire both at once.

## DECEMBER 27

One while we do not wonder that so many commit suicide, life is so barren and worthless; we only live on by an effort of the will. Suddenly our condition is ameliorated, and even the barking of a dog is a pleasure to us. So closely is our happiness bound up with our physical condition, and one reacts on the other. Do not despair of life. You have no doubt force enough to overcome your obstacles. Think of the fox prowling through the wood and field in a winter night for something to satisfy his hunger. Notwithstanding cold and the hounds and traps, his race survives. I do not believe any of them ever committed suicide.

## DECEMBER 28

Unjust laws exist: shall we be content to obey them, or shall we endeavor to amend them, and obey them until we have succeeded, or shall we transgress them at once? Men generally, under such a government as this, think that they ought to wait until they have persuaded the majority to alter them. They think that, if they should resist, the remedy would be worse than the evil. But it is the fault of the government itself that the remedy *is* worse than the evil. *It* makes it worse. Why is it not more apt to anticipate and provide for reform? Why does it not cherish its wise minority? Why does it cry and resist before it is hurt? Why does it not encourage its citizens to be on the alert to point out its faults, and do better than it would have them? Why does it always crucify Christ, and excommunicate Copernicus and Luther, and pronounce Washington and Franklin rebels?

RESISTANCE TO CIVIL GOVERNMENT

## DECEMBER 29

These motions everywhere in nature must surely be the circulations of God. The flowing sail, the running stream, the waving tree, the roving wind,—whence else their infinite health and freedom? I can see nothing so proper and holy as unrelaxed play and frolic in this bower God has built for us. The suspicion of sin never comes to this thought. Oh, if men felt this they would never build temples even of marble or diamond, but it would be sacrilege and prophane.

## DECEMBER 30

I am reminded by my journey how exceedingly new this country still is. You have only to travel for a few days into the interior and back parts even of many of the old States, to come to that very America which the Northmen, and Cabot, and Gosnold, and Smith, and Raleigh visited. If Columbus was the first to discover the islands, Americus Vespucius and Cabot, and the Puritans, and we their descendents, have discovered only the shores of America. While the Republic has already acquired a history world-wide, America is still unsettled and unexplored. Like the English in New Holland, we live only on the shores of a continent even yet, and hardly know where the rivers come from which float our navy. The very timber and boards and shingles of which our houses are made, grew but yesterday in a wilderness where the Indian still hunts and the moose runs wild.

THE MAINE WOODS

## DECEMBER 31

Every one has heard the story . . . of a strong and beautiful bug which came out of the dry leaf of an old table of apple-tree wood, which had stood in a farmer's kitchen for sixty years, first in Connecticut, and afterward in

Massachusetts,—from an egg deposited in the living tree many years earlier still, as appeared by counting the annual layers beyond it; which was heard gnawing out for several weeks, hatched perchance by the heat of an urn. Who does not feel his faith in a resurrection and immortality strengthened by hearing of this? Who knows what beautiful and winged life, whose egg has been buried for ages under many concentric layers of woodenness in the dead dry life of society, deposited at first in the alburnum of the green and living tree, which has been gradually converted into the semblance of its well-seasoned tomb,—heard perchance gnawing out now for years by the astonished family of man, as they sat round the festive board,—may unexpectedly come forth from amidst society's most trivial and handselled furniture, to enjoy its perfect summer life at last! I do not say that John or Jonathan will realize all this; but such is the character of that morrow which mere lapse of time can never make to dawn. The light which puts out our eyes is darkness to us. Only that day dawns to which we are awake. There is more day to dawn. The sun is but a morning star.

WALDEN

# THOREAU'S WRITINGS

*Collected Essays and Poems*, Elizabeth Hall Witherell, ed. New York: Library of America, 2001.

*Faith in a Seed*, Bradley P. Dean, ed. Washington, DC: Island Press, 1993.

*Letters to a Spiritual Seeker*, Bradley P. Dean, ed. New York: W.W. Norton & Company, 2004.

*A Week on the Concord and Merrimack Rivers*, *Walden*, *The Maine Woods*, *Cape Cod*, Robert F. Sayre, ed. New York: Library of America, 1985.

*Wild Fruits*, Bradley P. Dean, ed. New York: W.W. Norton & Company, 2000.

*The Writings of Henry David Thoreau*, 20 vols. Boston: Houghton Mifflin Company, 1906.